Tiara!
You're mad
and you'll alu
my girl. hope you
Dad

PRAISE FOR
THE VALUE EQUATION

"So much organizational value is lost today because many business owners are not leading their businesses with clear and compelling core values. This is an insightful book on the importance of managing a company with care, integrity, and wisdom. Leading from these values is common sense but too often not common practice. Garry and Steve have done a great job in clearly demonstrating the significant business value that can be achieved by aligning your core values to your daily business practices. Avoid the mistakes of thousands of other business leaders—read this book and you will significantly impact your organization."

—**Richard Fagerlin, Founder and President,
Peak Solutions**

"This is an insightful book on the importance of managing a company with care and integrity and wisdom. *The Value Equation* is a revelation, not because we don't know this, but because we don't intentionally practice this. Garry and Steve are on the front end of a major new way of doing business with this book. Highly recommended."

—**Carl Lee, Author, Speaker, VC and CEO,
CartoPac International**

"Everyone talks about values-aligned leadership, but few explain how to figure your values out and how to align your organization with those values. *The Value Equation* does just that. In a systematic fashion, the authors take the reader through the essential process of aligning your values with your organizational leadership. Well written and a fun read while guiding you to this most essential alignment."

—**Dr. Gary W. Ewen, Dean of the School of Business
and Leadership at Colorado Christian University**

"In *The Value Equation*, Garry and Steve give us not only a well-articulated argument on the importance of aligning our core values to our business outcomes, but they give us a nice process tool kit as well. Very thought provoking and an enjoyable read."

—**Paul Davis, CEO, Intricate Systems**

"*The Value Equation* underscores how important it is to align our business practices with our own core values. Garry and Steve are strategic and action orientated in defining a much-needed process. This book is inspiring, thought provoking and well written."

—**Drew Yancey, CEO Yancey's Food Service and Ph.D. candidate, University of Birmingham**

"The foundation of a healthy life is knowing who you are and what you believe—your core values. *The Value Equation* teaches that success comes from living your values, in both business and personal life."

—**Bob Walker, President, Walker Manufacturing, Inc.**

"*The Value Equation* is a 'must apply' for any entrepreneur, operator, or business manager. The insights and practical applications gained are relevant to all sizes and stages of business. I am impressed by how Garry and Steve organize and pragmatize the essentials while demonstrating how to align actions with values to create value. I only wish I had read this earlier in my career."

—**Dan Pellegrino, Managing Director, The Forbes M+A Group**

"*The Value Equation* speaks to intrinsic issues that deep down inside many business owners know but struggle to recognize, communicate, and use to guide their business strategies and daily operations. Garry and Steve have developed a succinct and understandable framework along with easy-to-use processes to identify core values, and prioritize and implement transformative actions that can promote business (and personal) success and contentment. This is a valuable and challenging read, and an excellent reminder to commit one's life and life work to things that really matter!"

—**Andrew Stewart, President, EDM International, Inc.**

THE VALUE EQUATION

ALIGN YOUR CORE VALUES

TRANSFORM YOUR BUSINESS

CREATE SUSTAINABLE SUCCESS

GARRY KRUM

WITH

STEVEN SMITH

The Value Equation
Align Your Core Values, Transform Your Business, and Create Sustainable Success

By Garry Krum with Steven Smith © 2018

All rights reserved. Use of any part of this publication, whether reproduced, transmitted in any form or by any means, electronic, mechanical, photocopying, recording, or otherwise, or stored in a retrieval system, without the prior consent of the publisher, is an infringement of copyright law and is forbidden.

While the publisher and author have used their best efforts in preparing this book, they make no representations or warranties with respect to the accuracy or completeness of this book and specifically disclaim any implied warranties of merchantability or fitness for a particular purpose. No warranty may be created or extended by sales representatives or written sales materials. The advice and strategies contained herein may not be suitable for your situation. You should consult with a professional where appropriate. Neither the publisher nor the author shall be liable for any loss of profit or any other commercial damages, including but not limited to special, incidental, consequential, or other damages. The stories and interviews in this book are true although the names and identifiable information may have been changed to maintain confidentiality.

The publisher and author shall have neither liability nor responsibility to any person or entity with respect to loss, damage, or injury caused or alleged to be caused directly or indirectly by the information contained in this book. The information presented herein is in no way intended as a substitute for counseling or other professional guidance.

Hardcover ISBN: 978-1-61206-153-5
Softcover ISBN: 978-1-61206-154-2
eBook ISBN: 978-1-61206-155-9

Cover Design by: inJoy Design, inJoy-Design.com
Interior Design by: Fusion Creative Works, FusionCW.com
Lead Editor: Jennifer Regner

For more information, visit www.AgoraConsulting.us.

To purchase this book at highly discounted prices, go to AlohaPublishing.com or email alohapublishing@gmail.com.

Published by

AlohaPublishing.com

Printed in the United States of America

To our clients—past, present, and future.

CONTENTS

Introduction: Why the Value Equation?   **13**

How do you fix entrepreneur anxiety? And besides the lack of revenue or other obvious problems, what causes it? If what you achieve in your business is not in line with the values that are important to you, you may feel unsatisfied, unhappy with where your business is going.

Chapter 1: What's Driving You and Your Business?   **23**

Do you know what your values are—what is important to you—and how they relate to your reasons for being in business? You can influence your own actions and reactions based on your core values—when you know what they are and how to express them.

Chapter 2: Understanding Your Core Values   **45**

Companies continually demonstrate their values through their products and services, through their customer, employee, and community relationships . . . often to their lasting success—or their imminent peril. Understand your personal and business values so you can focus your business to express them.

Chapter 3: Painting a Picture of Success   59

What values do you want to create through your personal life and business? Define your values, describe what that life and business would look like, and then plan how you will get there. A picture only comes to life when you execute, deliver and accomplish what you *plan* to do.

Chapter 4: Assessments—Knowing Where You Are   73

Use Assessments to see where you are. The Values Assessment Scorecard gives you the opportunity to evaluate how well you are delivering and living out your core values in and through your business. The Business Assessment Scorecard shows where you need to prioritize your efforts in aligning your business practices to your core values.

Chapter 5: Identifying Critical Keys to Growth   87

You need to plan to succeed. Learn how to create a focused plan using Success Factors and Key Growth Factors and a simple 100-Day Plan to realize your goals. Align your core values, transform your business, and create sustainable success.

Chapter 6: Value-Aligned Leadership   105

The concepts covered here are not an exhaustive list, nor are they the last word on leadership. Yet, beyond any doubt, these seven concepts will have a huge effect on how you lead and will bring significant value and fulfillment to your life.

Chapter 7: Value Equation Stories of Success   121

What really happens when you experience the Value Equation process? Your business's focus would not be about making money or profit. You would see your way to align your core values, transform your business, and create sustainable success that brings you great satisfaction and joy.

Epilogue: Rest—Value Restored   **139**

> Are you creating long-term, sustainable value in your business and your life? Joy, peace, innovation, credibility, integrity, love. Can you identify those things in your life that you really create? Is your life and work producing a sense of value, of fulfillment—or is it just stuff? Take time out to step back and think about your efforts and where they are taking you, to truly realize success in your life and business.

Recommended Reading	145
Appendix: The Value Equation Road Map	147
Acknowledgments	159
About Garry Krum	163
About Steven Smith	165
About Agora	167

We all demonstrate our values through how we live our lives.

Whether we become champions or villains or just ordinary people, we show others the important values in our lives through our actions.

Many business people don't stop to realize companies have distinct and identifiable values too. Companies continually demonstrate these values through their products and services as well as their customer, employee, and community relationships, which lead to lasting success or the collapse of brands.

Which will you be?

INTRODUCTION

WHY THE VALUE EQUATION?

> "Who a person is will ultimately determine if their brains, talents, competencies, energy, effort, deal-making abilities, and opportunities will succeed."
>
> —Henry Cloud, *Integrity*

Ian was an expert and remarkably knowledgeable woodworker. What gave Ian a competitive edge was his passion for creating something beautiful out of wood—consequentially he was constantly trying to develop new products. Ian started his manufacturing company over 15 years ago to make his passion a reality, instead of just a hobby. His new business allowed him to try new techniques and processes he never could have done in his garage. For the first 10 years, he created new and innovative products, identified and hired rising stars, and found a customer niche that allowed his revenue to grow. In short, he was living his passion.

Creating the company was a lot of work for Ian, but it was rewarding. However, after about 10 years the company started to hit

The Value Equation

a slump. Somehow, the revenue growth stalled. His approach and passion hadn't changed, yet his business wasn't operating as effectively as it had in the past. As his company had grown, he hired good managers and employees, but some of his rising stars had moved on to other jobs and some to competing companies. As replacement and new employees came onboard, Ian had a growing feeling that these new employees didn't share the same vision and passion as he did.

To make matters worse, profit margins were shrinking. He felt that he was losing customers and yet couldn't understand why—his products offered the same quality they had from the beginning, and he was able to keep costs competitive through new techniques that reduced production costs. Yet, Ian was increasingly uneasy . . . was his dream and all of his hard work coming to naught?

He spent his days looking for new markets for his products and researching competitively priced parts—which was not his strength, but he didn't want to hire anyone to do this for him. Ian was very worried about shrinking profits and started to focus on working harder to fix where he had gone wrong, though he wasn't really sure his remedies could fix it.

As he struggled, he no longer had the time to take vacations and generally didn't look forward to going to work—he feared he might lose everything he had worked for in his life. He often was unable to sleep and lay awake, night after night, puzzling through what wasn't working.

Does Ian's story sound familiar to you?

How Do You Fix Entrepreneur Anxiety?

The immediate question is how do you get off the merry-go-round of business frustration, anxiety, and dissatisfaction and start

Introduction

believing in your passion again? For a lot of business people, their frustration and anxieties lead them into attempts to take greater control over their business. Unfortunately, it's not just a matter of achieving control over your workplace, your business, or department . . . of being the boss. We don't need to tell you that just being the boss is not the answer.

If you are in this situation, you're not alone. A Gallup poll of entrepreneurs taken in 2014 showed that 57 percent like being an entrepreneur. They enjoy the freedom of "being the boss." Yet of those surveyed, only about **40 percent feel satisfied** with their business. That's 60 percent who are *not* satisfied.[1] Ironically, these are the business leaders who have the most control over their work environment—they own the company!

A lot of business professionals look for outside help. But most business consultants look at the most obvious and easy *symptoms* of the problem first, the easily quantifiable ones: lack of cash flow, insufficient working capital, flat revenues, inventory turn, good employees leaving for "better jobs or better opportunities," too many employee mistakes, loss of valued customers, etc. But these are not the real reasons for the frustrations—they are just the symptoms.

While the symptoms are varied, the impacts on business owners and executives are always the same—frustration, stress, fatigue, anger, fear, lack of time, and a loss of sleep. Very few of these business people can say they are really satisfied in their job or their business. This happens because they focus on day-to-day work issues and problems that don't lead them to what's really important.

And then the merry-go-round continues. As a result, many hardworking business people and executives lose their passion alto-

The Value Equation

gether—maybe because the reasons they went into business are so far removed from what they do every day. The things they lay their hands on every day don't make a significant difference—and soon those things don't *matter* anymore.

They want to make that change, create something of worth, feel engaged in a larger purpose . . . feel as though they are making progress, yet their daily job gets disconnected from those goals.

> **What you achieve is not in line with the important values you want to create.**

The real problem—if this is you—is that the things you do every day are not aligned to the core values that enable the company to create worthy products and services for your customers, employees, vendors, and stockholders. It feels like a merry-go-round. You may be chasing the symptoms instead of looking at your company culture and how it is aligned to the foundational values you are trying to express and preserve. Remember, your business has values that customers see every day.

A foundational goal worth working for is to consistently deliver quality products that enrich the lives of your customers. Customer loyalty—the knowledge that your customers appreciate what you do and *want* to buy from you—is created when you revitalize your product or service quality and deliver excellent customer support. Focusing on a commitment to communication, integrity, and truth are *values* that create employee loyalty and stability. You'll know you've arrived

Introduction

when your business starts to feel like a *community,* and your customers feel they are making a statement by buying from you.

> **You'll know you've arrived when buying from you makes a statement.**

You don't have to be perfect. No business is. But if you don't get the basics of discovering and aligning your foundational values to your business practices, then it's hard to get off the merry-go-round—and you'll struggle to find the satisfaction you crave, that feeling of accomplishment.

That's why we wrote *The Value Equation*. The Value Equation process can help you literally transform how you think and also how you *feel* about your business.

You'll start by focusing on creating exciting and practical values, not just chasing revenues or immediate profits. You'll stop focusing on the *money,* change your daily work, and align your processes so they are aimed at achieving your foundational goals—those reasons you went into business. You'll regain that sense of excitement and adventure by focusing on creating sustainable value around the things that *matter.*

> **The solutions we articulate take time and discipline. If you want to see real and lasting success, you must be intentional and focused. The results will come . . . Yet it is ultimately up to you to start.**

The Value Equation

Finding Value, Every Day

We understand that transformations are not easy. We live in a crazy, fast-paced world that is accelerating the demands on businesses just to survive. Technology is constantly creating opportunities and obstacles, people become polarized when they can't see a solution, and government regulations drive many people beyond their patience. New generations have been born into the rise of terrorism and experienced global recessions and expansions, and they are bombarded by reports of climate change.

> **As a society, we simply can't take the values we grew up with for granted. We need to reconfirm those values if they are to remain relevant.**

How you work in your business every day can be a part of how those values are expressed—to your employees, your vendors, and your customers. Creating a little calm, order, and meaning in this chaos will require **clarity of purpose, alignment with values, and actions driven by purposeful intent.**

Value Versus Values

Before we go too much farther, we need to lay some foundations. We use the words *value* and *values* a lot in this book. By **value**, we generally mean something that's important in a significant way or something that has worth or importance—something that you can generally measure.

Introduction

Values, on the other hand, are the beliefs, principles, and ethics you hold important in your life. In business, of course you want to create measurable value—great customer loyalty, good company morale, a reasonable profit, etc. However, if you create value but that value is not in alignment with your internal and company values, you can lose your passion and purpose. We will have more to say on this in later chapters.

What Can the Value Equation Mean for You?

The Value Equation is about business success. But it turns out that your personal values need to be a part of your business life too. They are what distinguishes you from your competitors and they are a big part of your *why*—those reasons your customers will love buying from you. They are also what makes you love what you do every day. And when you can communicate those values to your customers, your employees, and your vendors, success will come because they all know what you stand for and they want to be a part of it.

We want to show you how to define, articulate, and create success by aligning your daily activities with your foundational business values.

The more your actions are aligned with your goals and values, the better chance you have of creating success.

The Value Equation Process

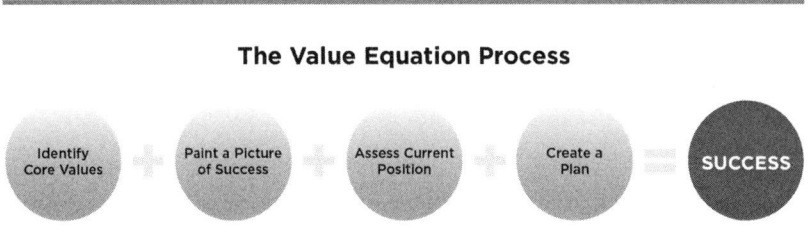

The Value Equation

The Value Equation process starts by ***identifying*** what's important to you. We'll help you clarify and articulate which values you need to express for your success.

Then we'll show you how to develop an intentional value-building plan by ***painting a picture*** of what success can look like down the road—honestly ***assessing*** your current situation and identifying the values you want to live and work by. We'll show you some simple but powerful tools to help you align your efforts with a plan for successful results.

Then we will outline important areas of leadership and management as they apply to aligning your values with your business practices. We'll address the clarity with which you speak, the vision you communicate, and the leadership you demonstrate—and how these issues are critical to your success and the fulfillment of your goals. The more your employees and other stakeholders embrace your vision and values, the more success you and they will create and share.

> **The Value Equation process has multiple steps with one singular focus in mind: to help businesses find enduring success by aligning their business practices to their core values.**

You can transform the way you think and act in your business. Transform your business delivery, your products and services, the way you sell, and how you manage your employees. But understand, it is a transformation that starts with *you*, and then your business. That is what this book is about—helping you develop a way of seeing that will help you *align* and *thrive*.

Introduction

While this book focuses on business people and processes (entrepreneurs, small and mid-cap companies, nonprofit organizations, large corporations, governmental organizations, etc.), the Value Equation process is also relevant to the individual life. As you work through the process, think about how your life would be affected if you aligned your personal actions with your fundamental values at work and at home. The incredible power of the Value Equation is a process to help you make those alignments. It's relevant to your life and your organization.

Notes

1. Gallup Poll, September 30, 2014.

WHAT'S DRIVING YOU AND YOUR BUSINESS?

> "If you ask most businesses why their customers are their customers, most will tell you it's because of superior quality, features, price or service. In other words, most companies have no clue why their customers are customers."
>
> —Simon Sinek, *Start with Why*

Motivation and Daily Mojo

Here is the real secret to this process: Even though you are in business to sell—to create revenue—what motivates you (and your employees, your vendors, and your customers) isn't money. It's the meaning behind what you do.

We are not alone in believing this. Most psychologists tell us that humans have two deep desires. One is the need for intimacy and second, a need for a life that has value or *meaning*—significance. We can strive to obtain intimacy and significance through a combination of avenues: through relationships, religious commitments and

The Value Equation

beliefs, charitable giving or nonprofit work, creative hobbies, and sports outlets, for example.

As it turns out, these basic motivations are important to the workplace—for leaders and followers. People, to varying extents, view their position at work and what they spend their time doing there as part of their identity. It's part of how they *show up*. Generational differences affect people's attitudes and expectations about their work, but fundamentally, nearly everyone feels great about working for a company that makes a difference and stands for something worth talking about.

And we are seeing an increased emphasis on these motivations. In the twenty-first century workplace, the millennial generation, which is eclipsing the Gen Xers, is starting to dominate. Millennials have been characterized as being more concerned about workplace satisfaction than just monetary compensation. A work-life balance is considered essential. They are less likely to put up with an unpleasant work environment or lack of a real company message than previous generations. Generation Z workers, as they enter the workforce, are expected to accelerate these tendencies.

And customers are changing as well. Customers are becoming more aware and more likely to research product information through the internet and social media than ever before. Brand names are proven through customer satisfaction ratings in the online marketplace. While discounting prices is still a significant marketing and sales tactic, price alone is no longer a viable approach. Your company, to truly be successful, needs to *stand for something*. Your customers need to know *why* you are in business.

What's Driving You and Your Business

Social media has given a voice to anyone who wants to speak. If a business does not consistently deliver its products and services as advertised, the downfall of a brand can be quick and dramatic. To be consistent and maintain success, the alignment of business values to business practices must be completely in sync.

Two well-known American companies have effectively created and communicated messages that enabled their success and defined their *why*: Apple, Inc., and Southwest Airlines.

How to Do the *Why*

There are several well-known examples of companies that everyone just "gets" what they stand for. Apple has demonstrated their core values of innovation, design, and intuitive ease of use by introducing integrated products such as the iPhone, iPad, and iPod, specifically building new capabilities across market segments (phones, music, watches, laptops, etc.). Price is no longer the driving factor in the rollout of successive new products because they are now demonstrating they no longer operate in the old markets. They have created significant new capabilities (value) by integrating markets.

Southwest Airlines grew by combining a strategy of low-cost fares *plus* on-time performance (quality) achieved through no-frills flights . . . and these values were clear and consistent to everyone.

Aligning your core values to your business processes is important for achieving success. To reach your customers, you must visibly align your company messaging and online presence. This is critical for maintaining and sustaining the success of your business for that growing segment of society that desires transparency, honesty, quality, and product/company loyalty. This new consumer model is slowly replacing the twentieth-century discount pricing models that drove consumers to seek out the lowest price, regardless of quality or reputation.

Both Apple and Southwest Airlines achieved full integration of their values in interactions with customers and vendors as well employees, managers, and stockholders. Clarity, communication, and consistently demonstrating their values were key for both of these companies to keep company processes aligned to their values and goals. Their ability to "walk the talk" as a business entity—in short, providing products and services in line with their company identity, stated values, and demonstrated business practices—was critical to their sustained success.

Before you can align your business to your values, you need to know what they are. If you've never thought about this, the values you want to express in your business may not be obvious to you. What are *your* core values? What are the core values of your business? Are these the same values your customers see?

Beyond Basic Needs—More Than Survival

Basic human needs and values have been studied intensely—those critical requirements for life and fulfillment. Abraham Maslow is perhaps the most recognized for defining five levels of basic human needs:

- physical survival
- physical safety
- love and belonging
- self-esteem
- self-fulfillment or self-actualization

What's Driving You and Your Business

Maslow's logic assumed that if you can survive and find safety, then you can build other life fulfillment-type needs.[1] Shalom Schwartz later took this concept further and identified 10 distinct motivational values in his *The Theory of Basic Human Values*.[2] He broke down human fundamental values into four higher-order groups:

- conservation
- openness to change
- self-enhancement
- self-transcendence

Using Schwartz's work, we outlined a set of hierarchical core values (or drivers) and applied them to business operations. This hierarchy makes it easy to categorize the values you want to express in your business.

The Value Equation Hierarchy

Our simple hierarchy of personal and business values fits into three building blocks: survival, identity, and enrichment values.

1. **Survival values.** Having the economic and social resources to eat, drink, reproduce, and fend off foes.
    - **For business:** income, productivity, efficiency, competence.
    - **For people:** companionship, provision, health.
2. **Identity values.** Having a primary sense of value and purpose.
    - **For business:** brand identification, customer loyalty, market differentiation, effectiveness, communication, consistency, transparency.
    - **For people:** love, faith, honesty, friendship, courage, integrity, empathy.

The Value Equation

3. **Enrichment and enjoyment values.** Allowing true fulfillment and enjoyable existence.
   - **For business:** belief in company, loyalty, vision, creativity.
   - **For people:** fun, peace, freedom, variety, adventure.

The chart below graphically shows the hierarchy of these values as three levels.

Personal and Business Values Hierarchy

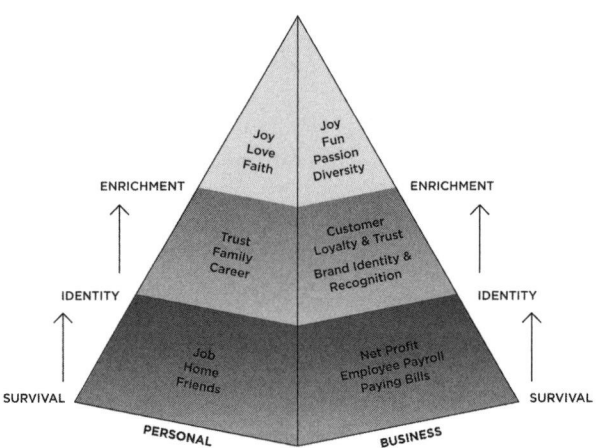

Level I: Survival

You spend a lot of your life working—most of your time is spent trying to create a living to support yourself and your family. Companies focus on the basics . . . sales revenue, inventory, cost of sales or services, financial statements, bank loans, employee relations, etc. Making payroll for employees and bank loan payments tends to get most of your attention.

> **Survival values are of primary concern for your business. They are also the motivation of fear-based management.**

What's Driving You and Your Business

The unfortunate side of the survival instinct is that it's primarily motivated by a sense of fear resulting from the expectation of a bad outcome: your best customer moves to your biggest competitor, the price of material raises dramatically, cash flow is tight and there may not be enough to make payroll.

When you get caught in this crazy trap of reaction, firefighting, and busyness, fear tends to dominate, and you then begin to operate your business out of that fear. A fear-based mentality has consequences—you begin to micromanage, lose trust in your employees, become manipulative in selling your products and services. Eventually you get stressed, lose sleep, and generally feel frustrated, unhappy, and angry.

Obviously, as an individual or as a company, you need to survive first before you can think about the next steps of planning your life, let alone thriving. But just keeping busy is not necessarily surviving.

At certain points in your life and work, you will probably get caught in the trap of tackling the issue or problem immediately in front of you . . . and taking some kind of action to keep busy appears to help. Other times, the problems and issues seem too complex to digest and you may just want to move forward in any way you can. So, you keep marketing and selling insurance policies, fixing the next broken auto, or making the next cabinet on the assembly line. Whatever you do . . . just *finish the next sale.*

The problem is when you are in that mode, you don't stop to think about where you are headed. You can get so lost in the maze of the day-to-day effort that you lose sight of the goal and simply focus on survival.

Fear: Chasing Results

The merry-go-round effort to just survive can generate actions based on short-term, reactive instincts and, more often, fear. It can drive business leaders to a behavior contrary to their own values, often without realizing they are chasing profits out of fear. Brad was no exception.

Brad was the owner of a manufacturing company. If asked, he would say that things were "okay." However, if you looked at his financial statements, you might disagree. For the last several years, revenue had stayed flat at $10 million a year and his gross profit margin had slowly dropped each year to less than 20 percent. Cash flow was tight because he went into debt to keep up with the slow times. Brad's business was slowly dying and under the surface, he was worried—very worried.

His survival solution was to chase revenue—just fill the queue with as much work as possible. Stay busy and somehow things would improve. So, he sat, day after day, answering requests for quotes, trying to keep everyone busy. Rather than looking at the fundamental problems of his business or addressing the primary reasons for why he was not growing, he sat in fear that he might lose it all and tried as hard as he could to answer as many bid requests as possible to keep his company busy. Worry, stress, trouble sleeping . . . fear!

Fear-Based Management Backfires

For Brad, the worst-case scenario was happening. In the midst of difficult times, delivery dates started to slip and quality begin to decline on the production line. At the recommendation of a local consultant, Brad installed a camera system to observe the shop activities in a desperate attempt to see what was going wrong.

Over the long term, workers need a safe environment to be creative, innovative, effective, and to sustain productivity.

You can imagine how that went over with the shop employees. Feelings of anger and resentment were immediate. They felt as though management was trying to control their every action. And what about creating a safe environment? Forget it. The result was a breakdown of trust and team cohesion, and productivity fell even more. It took a lot of time after the cameras came down for management to regain the trust of the workers. Eventually, team trust was reestablished and that, in turn, increased productivity and quality control in the shop. Living life out of fear does indeed have consequences.

Start by Recognizing Fear

Unfortunately, most critical problems **cannot** be solved by simply working more and trying harder. The solution is to recognize the fear reaction, honestly assess where your company stands, and then develop and execute a plan—a plan that addresses your current problems honestly, focuses on building a solid team, grows your sales, creates success—while staying aligned to your core values.

To do that, you need to get away from the fear solutions, the firefighting and reactive way of doing business and take the time to

The Value Equation

think. Time to look the problems in the eye and create a plan to deal with the real issues, time to create viable solutions, and realign your actions to your true values.

The first step in this path is to recognize fear driven symptoms and the alternatives. The chart below illustrates the behavioral characteristics of a fear-driven, reactionary company without a strategy versus one driven by planning and the creation of value.

Characteristics of Fear-Driven Companies

Fear-Driven	Plan- and Values-Driven
Confusion, reactive management	Clarity, purpose, proactive management
Lack of trust	Trust, teamwork
Controlling management, micromanagement	Freedom, independence, responsibility
Worry, stress	Confidence
Present focus, problem focus	Future focus, strategic focus
Low employee morale	High employee morale
High employee turnover	High employee loyalty and retention (making them nonrecruitable)
Poor or declining financial performance	Good financial results

Once you recognize these destructive survival traits, you can become aware of the perpetual problems and the internally generated circumstances that make the situation worse. Step back a bit . . . take a breath . . . get help . . . and act.

Maybe you are doing fairly well and your business is growing, you are making a fair profit, your employees seem happy—but still you feel like something is missing, that there's something more you could be doing. Making a good financial return and having enough working capital and a heathy balance sheet are wonderful, but temporary—**are you succeeding, but creating a negative wake in the process?**

What's Driving You and Your Business

Even financially successful companies need to be careful. Are you actually ensuring your long-term business success by creating what the customer sees as valuable products and services? Ones that create sustainable loyalty and company success?

Level II: Identity

Take a quick self-assessment. Do you win the discussion but leave negative feelings? Do your employees feel comfortable disagreeing with you? Are you building the success of your company based on value-aligned products/services, with content employees who understand the way forward, vendors who go the extra mile to ensure your demands are met, and customers who choose your business as a first recourse?

Once you can sit back and start thinking about the future of your work, an obvious question emerges. What are your goals, your *values*—those reasons you went into business in the first place? Those things you want to be known for, that you want others to know they will get when they work with you and buy from you.

To really take stock of what you represent and where you want to go, it's best to evaluate *where you are*. You can do this in a variety of ways, primarily through internal and external assessments. Be careful and prepared to be emotionally mature—you may be surprised by both the negative and positive reviews. However, the key to gaining insight into where you need to go is to first *honestly assess* where you are and how others see you—not what you think they should see. Do others see your business identity the same way you do?

The Value Equation

> **You can influence your own actions and reactions based on your core values— when you know what they are and how to express them.**

Part of your company message is your identity—those values that define who you are. Like Apple and Southwest Airlines, many businesses have successfully identified unique and differentiating strategies that are aligned to their core values.

There are also companies that have struggled but succeeded after firmly identifying and aligning their core business values to company business processes. Harley Davidson is a company that has created a following based on their representation of freedom and independence. Walt Disney is known for innovation in providing a family fantasy experience; Patagonia, for their environmental awareness and attention to functional quality; and Amazon, for continuous evolution of product lines and innovative shopping experiences.

These companies differentiated themselves from their competitors in these ways:

1. They launched memorable product and services that provided value to others—and they exceeded customer expectations.
2. They brought unique products and services to market.
3. They knew their customer base well—and *anticipated* what their customers wanted.
4. They had strong leaders who were committed to excellence and the delivery of their company's core values.

What's Driving You and Your Business

5. They had passion for their products, services, and for standing out from the crowd.

Develop or Change Your Identity . . . While Creating a New Plan

But all this success *started with a plan.*

Most private business owners and many larger company executives have little idea where they are headed. Studies and the observations of our Agora team show that 90-95 percent of private businesses have no business plan.[3] That is, they have no clearly articulated goals or a plan to grow—no clear path to success. Their operations are focused on day-to-day survival.

Take this quick three-question survey of your workplace (or yourself): Most people can't clearly state *why* they do what they do.

1. Do you and your coworkers, leaders, employees (or friends) know what your company's (and your) most important values are . . . and how those values are expressed through their work (or your life)?
2. Does your company clearly define what "success" looks like, other than profit? (Do your friends know what success looks like for you?)
3. When was the last time your company values were communicated to your employees, vendors, and customers—and not as some obtuse mission statement?

Based on your answers to these questions, do you know where you are going and why? If it seems clear that you don't—how are

The Value Equation

you going to create any significant, lasting value if you don't know where you are going and what you are creating?

But you can change that.

Without a clear plan that validates core values, your business is just living day to day, reacting to the demands of your immediate situation. Without clarity, your business is running *you*. A friend of mine once said that "our businesses are perfectly positioned to achieve the results we are getting," meaning that if you want different results, you must change the way you manage to get them.

Financially successful and sustaining companies are careful . . . yes, they take risks, innovate with new products, and take failure as indicators, not crushing setbacks. But they are also careful not to believe that past success guarantees future profits. Making reasonable money is great, but is your business creating long-term success by continually ensuring your values are being upheld and renewed? In other words, you need to regularly evaluate where you are and whether what you are doing still works—or needs to adapt to changing conditions.

Level III: Enrichment

Doing It Right

So, what does a company look like when its values, practices, and financial success are all working in alignment? Here are a few excellent businesses that put considerable focus on living out their values.

Patagonia

When Yvon and Malinda Chouinard set out to build Patagonia, they had a set of values they wanted to create and achieve through

What's Driving You and Your Business

their business—producing quality, functional outdoor products, while taking care of the environment and having fun! They succeeded in making exceptional and great-looking products, they used care in their manufacturing processes, and they continue to give one percent of their gross sales to environmental organizations. And they didn't forget the fun . . . for example, many of their corporate employees hit the waves when the surf's up in Ventura, California.

They didn't know what they were doing, completely, when they started the business back in 1973, but they did know that they wanted to do it right. When Yvon started making climbing gear, he created higher quality, more functional pitons and carabiners than the existing competition. When he realized the pitons were damaging to the rock walls of Yosemite, he switched to "clean" climbing gear and his business went ballistic.

The first functional clothing Yvon sold—heavy, Scottish corduroy knickers and English rugby shirts—were solid, durable, and all the rage in Yosemite Valley. Their first pile jackets were warm and efficient, even if they were a bit ugly when well used and dirty! Still, they were the most ubiquitous jackets around climbing circles. Today, you are more likely to see a Patagonia jacket on the streets of Paris than on Mont Blanc. And that's not because it's the best-looking jacket around; Patagonia jackets make a statement.

Everybody respects Patagonia because of what Patagonia stands for and what they do. It's not just great products, but the social values as well. Their actions were always aligned to their core values—the values they considered critically important to life and business.

It takes a leader to coalesce disparate perspectives and desires into a clear and articulate vision for the future. Yvon and Malinda Chouinard shared that vision for Patagonia with the insight and

The Value Equation

tenacity that made their products desirable and valued. This kind of value-aligned success usually starts with an individual desire—a personal vision that leverages the company for something greater than just money and profits.

Harley-Davidson

Simon Sinek (*Start with Why: How Great Leaders Inspire Everyone to Take Action*)[4] describes the alignment of business purpose with core values as intrinsic to discovering *why* the company exists and the success this brings. He uses Harley-Davidson as a prime example of a company that manufactures quality but more importantly, they inspire the consumer by delivering something more—a sense of the values they have identified and choose to represent. And by buying those products, their customers communicate what *they* choose to represent.

Harley-Davison has developed an incredible culture as the "Harley Way of Life," epitomized by independence and freedom, open sky, skullcaps, and a snarky attitude. Harley-Davidson riders have a brand loyalty something akin to the Marine Corps. They don't just ride the bike, they live the life—boots, jackets, tattoos, etc. Their motorcycles are ridden by motorcycle gangs, businessmen, and school teachers, all looking for more than a product. They are joining the Harley-Davidson sense of values—independence, a rebellious attitude, and belonging to the Harley community.

Companies and organizations succeed primarily because they have a clear understanding of the values they are building and an intentional plan to align and deliver those values. In northern Colorado, we are blessed with companies and organizations like OtterBox, Walker Manufacturing, and even our local symphony orchestra, that believe in delivering value.

What's Driving You and Your Business

OtterBox

OtterBox is the well-known maker of high-quality protective cases for cell phones and other electronics. I remember sitting in a room with the OtterBox executive team, asking about how protective their phone cases *really* were. I had just bought an OtterBox case and I was curious about some of the crazy stories I had heard about their product testing. Suddenly, a member of their team grabbed *my* phone and threw it against a concrete wall across the room! He went over and picked it up, handed it back to me and said, "You tell me what you think." A little panicked, I looked at my phone. Nothing. No scratches, no dings, no damage. It was working perfectly.

Confidence. The OtterBox team not only believed in their product quality but were willing to prove it as well. The case was not just a piece of plastic wrapped around a phone. It was highly engineered to withstand significant impact and manufactured to those engineering specifications. They knew and had confidence in their products—based on actual design and testing, not just hope. This laser focus on delivering high quality (and crazy testing) has produced success.

Walker Manufacturing

Bob Walker, the President of Walker Manufacturing, is an unusual man. Walker Manufacturing produces high-end lawn mowers, primarily used by professional lawn care companies worldwide. So, you would think that Bob would be a busy man. Yet Bob has a practice of returning every phone call, every email, and every text message he receives within 24 hours. He even returns calls to cold callers and strangers.

The Value Equation

Bob places value on people. He believes that people matter. Everything that Walker Manufacturing does is in alignment with this core value. Employees, vendors, retailers, customers, *everyone*. Bob's and his company's core values are aligned to their business practices, almost to a fault.[5] This is the primary reason for the success of his family business.

Fort Collins Wind Symphony

The local wind symphony in Fort Collins, Colorado, not only delivers high-quality musical performances, but they do it with panache and a great spirit of fun. Whether it is a serious performance, a Beethoven symphony, or a lighthearted evening of movie scores, they are aligned to the value of giving memorable performance experiences. These enjoyable performances are free to the public—yet they have a significant number of season supporters that embrace their style and values and make the symphony and their concerts possible.

In addition, the symphony supports the musical education of young people in the community. With the tight budgets of the local school districts, music education gets limited support. The symphony's role here is critical, by providing support to student concerts, music and performance lessons, and supplemental support to the small number of school music teachers.

Each of these businesses have created success—far beyond the borders of northern Colorado—because they knew their values and had a plan to align those values to their business plans and operations.

What's Driving You and Your Business

Characteristics of Northern Colorado Businesses

OtterBox	Walker Manufacturing	Fort Collins Wind Symphony
Golden rule Treat others the way you want to be treated.	Respect for employees and their families.	Making a substantial contribution to the musical life of members and patrons.
Passion A burning desire to win.	Keep promises and pursue excellence.	Giving audiences memorable performance experiences.
Innovation Have the courage to find new ways to solve life's problems.	Lead by serving.	Assist in the music education of young people.
Integrity Do the right thing, the right way, even when no one is watching.	Always love people.	Provide members with an opportunity for musical expression, growth, and fellowship.
Giving back To whom much is given, much is expected. We grow to give.	Manufacturing with integrity.	And fun, don't forget the fun!

There are numerous engaging stories of value-aligned, successful businesses. It's part of making a success story. Look around your local community and you will find many examples of businesses and organizations delivering success by embracing and living out their values. Set your goals to align with your values. Develop a plan to succeed. Execute.

Doing It Wrong Is Obvious

The business world also has many examples of companies that struggle with the creation of values and misalignment of what they say versus what they do. All it takes is a quick look at today's business headlines to see this. United Airlines' customer services issues, Uber's leadership ethics and dishonesty, and VW's emissions scandal are just a few examples of larger companies caught doing it wrong in

The Value Equation

the media spotlight. Smaller companies might not make the news, but they struggle just the same. Unfortunately, many of us witnessed the collapse of local businesses due to greed during the Great Recession. No one has trouble identifying this, and the response is universal—stay away from them if you can.

Sometimes the "wrong" isn't so egregious that people avoid a company, but employee loyalty slips, sales tank, and the struggle for survival begins. This can happen with new leadership that takes a company in a different direction, without redefining their *why*. Simon Sinek described the Southwest Airlines of recent years as one of these. As the airline industry began to follow Southwest's lead, other airlines matched Southwest's business model. They didn't redefine their vision and lost their major differentiation appeal. While Southwest is still a good airline and retains many fans, they are no longer "the low-price leader."

Summary

We all have desires and values that we hold and enjoy—values that we can express in our businesses and in our personal lives. They define in many ways who we are and why we exist. They create stability, clarity, and significance . . . or the lack thereof.

We have argued the position that the clearer your values are and the more aligned your work and businesses are to those values, the more you maximize your chances of success and fulfillment.

In the next chapter, we will discuss how to know and understand your core values—how to find that clarity. These are the values you hold dear, the ones that get you up in the morning—and the ones that your employees and customers can embrace.

What's Driving You and Your Business

Notes

1. Maslow, Abraham. *A Theory of Human Motivation*. Martino Fine Books, 2013 (a reproduction of the original article).
2. See https://en.wikipedia.org/wiki/Theory_of_Basic_Human_Values for an explanation of Shalom H. Schwartz's theory in the field of intercultural research.
3. See Eric Wagner. "Five Reasons 8 out of 10 Businesses Fail." Forbes.com, September 12, 2016. Also "Succession Planning Study," PriceWaterhouseCooper, 2014.
4. Sinek, Simon. *Start with Why: How Great Leaders Inspire Everyone to Take Action*. Portfolio; Reprint edition, 2011.
5. Whitford, David. "How This Entrepreneur Works Christianity Into His Craft," Inc., July/August 2015. https://www.inc.com/magazine/201507/david-whitford/god-and-the-entrepreneur.html

2
UNDERSTANDING YOUR CORE VALUES

> "To become a credible leader, you have to comprehend fully the deeply held beliefs, values, principles, standards, ethics and ideals that drive you. You have to freely and honestly choose the principles you will use to guide your decisions and actions... You must authentically communicate your beliefs in ways that uniquely represent who you are."
>
> —James Kouzes & Barry Posner, *The Leadership Challenge*

Let's go back to Ian's story. When Ian first started his company, there was enough demand for his products that he didn't need to differentiate what his company stood for or why he was in business. His high quality, lower cost products developed a word-of-mouth reputation that was enough to *sustain* success against competition. But somewhere along the way, the world had changed, and he no longer stood out from his competitors.

After internally fretting over his business, Ian eventually took action. He knew he was losing competitiveness and started to be-

The Value Equation

lieve his market niche had changed, and that he needed to change to compete. So, he started to offer his wood products at lower prices and began competing in lower-price markets. This new market niche required higher-production outputs with lower-quality products—Ian was chasing price.

Unfortunately for Ian's company, his production techniques and skilled workers weren't established for low-cost, high-production outputs. His remaining original employees and his older managers were starting to get disillusioned. Sales remained flat but profits were now seriously dropping. Things were getting worse. At this point, Ian reached out for help.

Value Equation Step 1:
Identify Your Core Values

The first thing we did was help him identify his core values—the motivations that generated his initial passion for his business. We helped him realize, as we worked through the Value Equation process, that those key values were critical to his initial success and he realized that was where his passion remained.

The Value Equation shown below highlights the first step in the process, ***identify core values.***

The Value Equation Process

Identify Core Values + Paint a Picture of Success + Assess Current Position + Create a Plan = SUCCESS

Understanding Your Core Values

A part of the new plan was to continue to evolve and strengthen his company's message of value and quality. He never really had to explain or express his values and message about long-term community and customer relationships, but now he realized it was an important part of his company that resonated with his quality products. He thought his 10-year-old website and trade magazine advertising was enough. In short, he was standing still while the world changed around him.

Once he had spent the time to identify his personal and core business values, he retooled his customer communications with his updated message. He refocused his products on quality, innovation, customer service, and flexibility to provide good product value. The response wasn't immediate, but it soon became clear that his customers weren't fading away as they had seemed to when he first sought help—they had just lost loyalty in the confusion Ian was struggling with. His company was beginning to find success again.

When you work to integrate your core values into your business and your goals, that transformational process converts what might be a mediocre business, just like your competitors, into lasting success. Values like independence, respect, humor, and creativity. It's not about chasing money, it's about creating value-added processes throughout your business that ensure success for your customers, employees, vendors, community, and stockholders—it's about providing benefits and improvements to the lives of everyone involved. Because of your values-aligned business, the profits will come—as will other unanticipated benefits. You'll see the impacts of these changes and how they will positively affect you and those around you.

The Value Equation

Ironically, as critical as this is, most owners and executives can't identify their basic business values beyond the financial outcomes from business, sales, and profit—those Level I survival values that everyone has. They may know their mission statement, but sales and profit are not values, they are benchmarks to measure if you are making an on-paper profit. You will never achieve your goals if you go into bankruptcy—so obviously making a profit has to happen first. So, what are the *values* we are talking about?

> **We all demonstrate our values through the way we live our lives. Whether we become heroes or villains, or for the most part just ordinary people, we show others the important values in our life through our actions.**

But most business men and women never stop to realize that **companies** have distinct and identifiable values too.

Companies continually demonstrate their values through their products and services, through their customer, employee, and community relationships . . . often to their lasting success—or their imminent peril.

What Are Core Values?

In the introduction, we briefly discussed the difference between *value* and *values,* with an "s." These differences are important.

One dictionary's definition of **value** is something having worth, merit, or importance, as in having financial value or comparative

Understanding Your Core Values

value. A value can also be something you hold in regard or esteem highly, like friendship or a new car. Value as we define it is multifaceted and varied, depending on your context. Businesses create value through the sales of quality products and services. You value your good customers, your loyal employees, and your supportive vendors. In a simplistic sense, business is essentially the exchange of value (a product) for value (money).

Tim Koller, Richard Dobbs, and Bill Huyett (McKinsey & Company), in the book *Value,*[2] describe business value as driven by business growth, return on capital, and the resulting cash flows. It is readily identifiable, quantifiable and, for business objectives, can be described in financial terms like gross profit and net income.

Yet, we also understand artistic value—the demand and value artwork generates because of its inherent beauty, innovation, and uniqueness. Intimacy is of significant value, and so is our health, education, financial stability, and even fun. Spiritual value is very personal and, like artistic value, may have a subjective meaning and worth to each individual.

Values, on the other hand, make up your character, beliefs, ethics, and morals. They are the components of your internal guidance system and motivational compass . . . they are not simply your desires, but your internal system of controls and motivators. Values have a major influence on your behavior and attitude and serve as broad guidelines in all situations. Some common business values are fairness, innovation, competence, and community involvement. Your personal values tell you not to harm others intentionally (kindness, love) or not to be cruel or dishonest.

The Value Equation

Values, in the sense that we use the term, are extremely varied and complex. They are the identity and enrichment values we described in the values hierarchy in the last chapter. Values can also be a bit more nebulous, and very personal. But as it turns out, they are much more critical to business success than you may think.

It is also important to note that as we all have personal values that guide us, businesses also have and live by their values. Look at any business and you can tell what kind of values they believe in by the way they create and deliver their products and services. Most business men and women don't realize that companies also have distinct and identifiable values. Companies continually demonstrate these values through their products and services, through their customer, employee, and community relationships . . . often to their lasting success *or* their imminent peril.

We also use the term ***core values***—these are the values that make you who you are, the values that are foundational to your life and that you hold dear. The following chart lists examples of core values that can be both personal and professional.

Some Examples of Core Values

Core Values			
Clarity	Love	Security	Joy
Sincerity	Forgiveness	Humility	Truth
Creativity	Diversity	Wisdom	Credibility
Kindness	Passion	Respect	Creativity

Your learned and intrinsic values may come from several sources. Your upbringing, religious influences, education, friends, the things you fear, and the things you enjoy or love.

Most of us obtain our sense of values from watching what our parents did well (or not so well) but also from school, religious be-

Understanding Your Core Values

liefs, friends, and even watching movies and TV. In your youth, the enrichment values may hold more importance for you than the identity values, but that's a personal thing and both can be motivational over your lifetime.

The relative importance of your values may also change over time. They get more mature and thoughtful and become more important to you—and some may be less important as life experiences, wisdom, and insight shape your values system. In fact, most of us move through life constantly making decisions through the lens of our values.

As an example of personal values, you might create a new product to grow a business, to feel accomplishment, to create financial value for yourself. You go on vacation to have fun, to escape the pressures of your job, and to rest. You might climb mountains for the challenge, the excitement, and to see beauty. Do you get excited and motivated when you are developing new and innovative products? These are enrichment values, entertainment values, but they can apply to both personal and business activities.

What about business values? Do you manage your employees to enhance their lives and treat your customers with respect? Do you trust your employees and allow them their own creativity and independence? Do you practice the same set of values at work as you do in your private life?

Everything you do should be driven by your values, and your values should drive everything that you do. These tend to be the identity values, the ones that impact your reputation and that of your business. Your identity values may look different in your personal life and your business, but they can stem from the same concept.

The Value Equation

Business values are the things that you work so hard to achieve. Your goal is not necessarily the money, it's the capability to provide quality and enrichment to customers, employees, and vendors through innovative products and services.

When you start changing customers' lives in meaningful and lasting ways, then you will know you've reached a level of enrichment, not just survival. It is not the size of your business that's important, it is the kind of impact you have on customers, employees, vendors, and your community.

Putting Your Core Business Values Into Action

Your core values are the most critical, foundational ones you have—your morals and ethics, your reputation, patriotism, independence, and helping the downtrodden are all examples of these. They are ideals and beliefs that you hold in high importance. The fulfillment of those ideas and beliefs, the creation and accomplishment of those values, are the most important things you can do in life. These values are your driving force, your motivation—the things that get you up and out of bed in the morning and keep you moving all day. They define who you are—your identity.

> Ben was a young executive, excited about taking over the family business. He was smart and creative with a good business head. He was so ready, and yet he was also nervous. He had demonstrated his abilities in an operational position, but taking over the business was a much bigger challenge.
>
> One of Ben's core values was respect. He wanted to be (and be seen as) capable, credible, and respected. He told me, "I just

Understanding Your Core Values

> want to know I can sit at the table." To him, that ability and answering that question for himself were huge. As we moved through the Value Equation process with Ben, we could see his talent for innovative business development ideas.
>
> We helped him develop and implement new strategies and services aimed at growing the business and improving gross profit margin. His people skills developed as did the respect others had for him. As the business grew, we could see his confidence as well as his capability and credibility improve. Results that followed our work together were the stuff of dreams: he took over the business, nailed the respect question, got married, has a new daughter, and the business is doing well.

It is critical that you understand yourself and understand what you truly value. What are your foundational values? Contentment, joy, influence, financial stability, integrity, truth? Understanding your core values is the critical first step, the foundation to building and sustaining success.

The **identity values,** the second level beyond basic needs, are your ultimate source of personal meaning and purpose. These also need to be lived out in your business. This expression of your identity through your work is important to people of all ages; it's a universal motivation that may often be expressed in reverse—that is, there are some kinds of work you won't do because they conflict with your values. When you find work that positively reinforces who you are, you have found true engagement and satisfaction in what you do every day.

The Value Equation

Simon Sinek writes, in his book *Start with Why*, that people don't buy *what* you sell, but *why* you sell what you sell. In other words, people embrace your business when they identify with your *why*, your identity values, because they value the same things.[1]

This makes sense. Your friends, for instance, for the most part share your same values. These can be both identity and enrichment values.

People naturally gravitate to those who live or play or vote or worship like they do. Yet do you give this idea much thought in business, in the sales of your products and services? Think about your best customers. Do they share your values, something in common that makes the sale easier? And that frustrating customer that seems to always be fighting you—perhaps your values conflict with theirs?

You may spend much of your free time working on your **enrichment** and **enjoyment values**. On a personal level, here is where you get to play. Yet, you will not feel successful and fulfilled if you can't also live out your enrichment values in your work and business. Fun, enjoyment, friendship, variety, peace, and freedom are all critical to being productive and capable.

Here's a basic question to answer: What are those lasting values that would enhance your business identity and significance? Can you provide clarification in your business by listing the business values that are not only clear to you, but also to your employees, customers, vendors, and stockholders? And can you do this in your life as well—that is, does your family truly know what you love to do?

Your employees, customers, and other stakeholders want clarity. They want a mission. They want to know the underlying purpose—*beyond the money*. They want to know your *why*. You can motivate

Understanding Your Core Values

yourself and a whole lot of other people if you know your mission and can clearly articulate it.

The first step in creating significant and lasting value in your organization is to think through and articulate your core values. What are they *really*?

Values aren't created because you desire them. They don't come into existence because you want them. They come into existence because you exercise, you demonstrate, you show, and you live those thoughts and desires and goals. Then they become part of your culture, and therefore they become your values. You create *value*—as in revenue and useful services and products that enhance your customer's lives and businesses—in a company by exercising those values and bringing more worth into your company and organizational activities.

Identifying Your Core Business Values

The frustration many business owners feel is in failing to achieve the values they really want to achieve, the ones that are in their soul. It's not that they're not making money. It's not because they have employee issues. Yes, those are real business issues and they need solutions, but they are not the real problem.

The deeper problem is that many business owners feel they are not achieving joy or fulfillment or . . . well, they aren't *having fun*. Because the results are not in alignment with their values, they are not happy. They're not achieving what they want to achieve. Their work feels empty.

The Value Equation

The question is . . . what values matter to you and your business? What values are at the core of who you are? *Why* do you do what you do?

Core Values Exercises

The two exercises below will help you examine and understand what really matters. Take time to do them. Don't rush—this is the most critical part of the Value Equation process. Give yourself plenty of time . . . a few hours over the next few weeks. Like most things in life, the more time you spend, the more return on your investment will come out of the process.

These two exercises may seem silly or soft, but it is critical that you understand yourself and what is of significant value to you. These are the values that you *must* create in your business. These are the values that will give your life more meaning. You may have never expected that these could be expressed in your working life—so you must look at who you are, beyond your work as it has been.

From the Heart: List Your Values

First, take a clean sheet of paper and list the values that are important to you. What values can you not live without? What are the things that create passion in you? What values do you find attractive in others? Think. Listen to your heart. Take enough time to list 10-15 values. Don't look at a list, just think about what is important to you.

Core Values Exercise

Second, do the Core Values Exercise: Download the list of 100 values from our website (www.AgoraConsulting.us). Print out the

Understanding Your Core Values

list and read through all of the values. Then cross out the values that aren't of critical importance to you. Yes, they are all important, but perhaps not to you. Then, circle the 20 most important to you. From that list of 20, choose the most important 10; then from those 10 choose the most critical five; then from those, choose one! For most people (including me), this is very difficult to get to one, but also enriching.

Now, compare the two lists. Do the two lists contain the same values? Is there a value that continues to resonate with you during these exercises? Redo the elimination of your lessor values using both lists. This will help reinforce your top core values. Take your time and enjoy the process.

Summary

Your core values are critical to who you are. These values define, to a large extent, your significance and purpose in life, but they are not just lived out in your personal life—they are also critical to building significant and lasting value in your business.

There are three types of values—survival, identity, and enrichment values.

There is also an important difference between *value*—something having worth (financial), merit, or importance, and *values*—the ideals that make up your character, beliefs, ethics and morals.

To find more fulfillment with your business, you need to identify and articulate your core values. This clarity not only gives you guidelines and support to determine a more intentional business focus, but also helps your employees, customers, suppliers, etc., embrace and align themselves with those values.

The Value Equation

To help with the identification and articulation of your values, we offer two simple exercises:

- An open-ended exercise in which you write, from your heart, 10-15 values on a clean sheet of paper without any prompting
- A Core Values exercise, in which you use a list of 100 values, that you can download from the tools section of our website, to identify your top core values: www.AgoraConsulting.us.

You will find this process fun and enjoyable, but also deeply rewarding. In this crazy, busy world we live in, we don't often allow ourselves the time for deep reflection. Knowing what is of importance to you allows you the ability to be much more intentional on living out those values rather than just reacting to your busy life. Who knows, perhaps this will start a trend!

In the next section, we will begin building a plan to help create and deliver your core values and business success.

Notes

1. Sinek, Simon. *Start with Why: How Great Leaders Inspire Everyone to Take Action*. Portfolio; Reprint edition, 2011.
2. Koller, Tim, Richard Dobbs, and Bill Huyett. *Value: The Four Cornerstones of Corporate Finance*. Wiley, 2010.

3
PAINTING A PICTURE OF SUCCESS

"When employees at all levels share a common understanding of where the company is headed, what success looks like, whom their competitors are, and what needs to be achieved to claim victory, there is a remarkably low level of wasted time and energy and a powerful sense of traction."

—Patrick Lencioni, *Four Obsessions of an Extraordinary Executive*

Karen was running a quilting business. Yet she didn't *want* to run a business! She came to us because what Karen wanted to do was teach quilting—that was her passion. Karen wanted to share the excitement of making quilts and using cool, innovative tools to help her customers cut patterns and pull fabrics into a finished quilt, quicker and easier. She found joy and fulfillment watching people get excited about creating quilts with her tools and techniques—that's what she loved.

However, she found herself spending 95 percent of her time running a business—ordering supplies, working with distributors,

The Value Equation

and managing employees. She wasn't happy, and the more time she spent away from teaching, the unhappier she became. She was stuck on the merry-go-round, frustrated that she wasn't able to do what she really wanted to do.

What she wanted to create and achieve—teaching the joy of quilting—was not in alignment with what she was actually doing. She was simply following the standard practices that she thought one did in a business, rather than thinking and implementing those things that created passion in her.

Through the Value Equation process, we helped her understand what she actually wanted to do and what values she genuinely wanted to create. It was a fun process because we completely changed her business. As a result, Karen's business and her outlook on what she did were transformed . . . she reorganized her business to emphasize teaching quilting techniques, and she rediscovered the fun and love of her passion . . . teaching. As a result, she is happier and making more money.

In this chapter, we will continue the discussion on the Value Equation and its methodology for creating significant and lasting value in your business. Now that you have begun to define your core values—what you would actually like to create through your business—you need to develop a plan to move from your current state of business to your desired state—where you really would like to be.

First, you need to define what success is. What does it look like? How will you know when you have succeeded? You need to get specific and articulate what you want to achieve. So let's start by painting a picture of what success looks like.

Painting a Picture of Success

The Value Equation shown below highlights the second step in the process: Painting a Picture of Success.

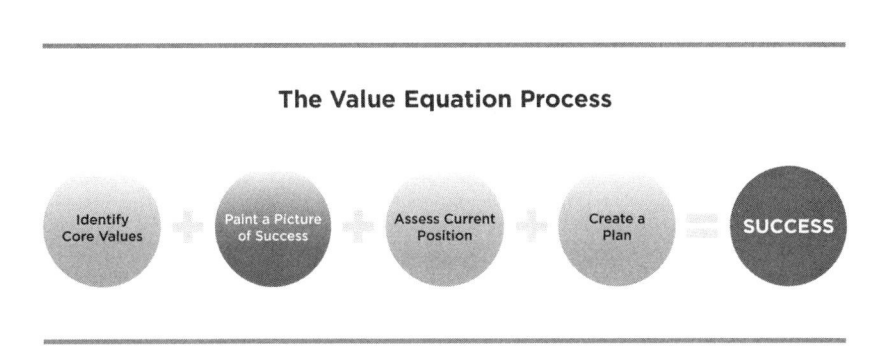

The Value Equation Process

Identify Core Values + Paint a Picture of Success + Assess Current Position + Create a Plan = SUCCESS

Value Equation Step 2: Painting a Picture of Success

Dream!

No, seriously, dream.

Look down the road and define what you would like to achieve. What values do you want to create through your personal life and business? What would your business look like, what would your life look like, and what would your business and your life be if you could just paint a picture from your imagination? So—dream, and really start to envision the future of your business and articulate that future.

You are about to do something that most people will never do—articulate a picture, a picture of success for their lives and their businesses! Most people just don't take the time. Yes, they may daydream, they may paint a picture of an exciting life they could live—but a picture only comes to life when you not only dream but also plan a course of action. When you execute, deliver, and accomplish what you *plan* to do.

The Value Equation

You need a picture in your mind (and on paper) to guide you and help you navigate the *why*—your purpose and goals. You also need to articulate, specifically, what those values and goals are.

> **First find your values, then describe what your life and business would look like with those values, and then plan how you will get there.**

Ask yourself questions. Think, daydream (with a purpose), write, and reflect on the future.

What does life look like in 10 years? What does your personal life look like? Personal goals, family, health, fun, education, lifestyle, etc. List those accomplishments—what sounds fulfilling to you? Then list the goals and accomplishments you would like to see for your life.

Picture your business five years down the road. Ask yourself open-ended questions like the ones below. Don't limit yourself to those questions. Take your time and play.

In five years . . .

- What will my company be best known for?
- What will set my company apart from the competition?
- What will my company's geographical reach be?
- What will my business look like, specifically—in terms of markets, market share, etc.?
- How much sales revenue will my company have?
- What new products or services will I be selling?

Painting a Picture of Success

- Who will my best customers be?
- What role will I be doing?
- Where will I be living?
- What will I give back to my community?
- Will my children be involved?
- What will my business legacy be?

Okay, I'll admit that for most business owners, this is very difficult. It is easier to just focus on the day-to-day details and not worry about the future.

> **You know the old saying, "Don't worry about tomorrow. Tomorrow will take care of itself." So don't worry . . . plan.**

You need to plan. You need to take the time and be creative. You and no one else is responsible for your future.

Success Factor Grid

Trying to paint a picture of what success looks like without some sort of guide can be difficult. At Agora, we use a *Success Factor Grid*, a tool to help you with this process. A Success Factor Grid (SFG) is a specific list of key items that define success—the things needed to achieve success. It is not a mission statement or a detailed business plan, but a clear, specific vision of what is desired, required, and critical to achieve success.

This process provides a clear road map of where you need to go. It marks a "stake in the ground." Through this process, you make

The Value Equation

specific decisions about *what* you value, given many others that you might have chosen, and interpret how it important those values are to you so others can understand them.

This is of huge importance, if done correctly. The creation of value starts with *you*. If you can't, as a leader or manager, be clear on the company's major goals and priorities, then how can you expect to create success? How will you know if and when you have reached it?

Paint the Picture

Let's start with your picture of life 10 years or so in the future. What would you like to accomplish during that period of time? Paint a picture by making a list of your big-picture goals and putting them into the following buckets of a Success Factor Grid (SFG):

1. Personal goals
2. Business goals
3. Financial goals
4. Legacy goals
5. Fun goals

Here is an example of what this might look like:

A Simple Picture of Success

Personal	Business	Financial	Legacy	Fun
Living a life of no regrets	Sales at $10M 15% net income	No debts	Reputation for integrity	Travel to all 50 states
Still in love . . .	40 loyal and happy employees	Own home	Community giving and involvement	Jump out of an airplane
Successfully launch the kids	Known as the place to buy . . .	Reasonable retirement resources	Providing meaningful jobs	Have one really crazy adventure!

This is a specific list of items that, if achieved, would *create success*. I chose to use five categories: personal, business, financial, etc.,

Painting a Picture of Success

but you could have one or many, depending on how broad or deep you want to go. I also listed only three items in each category. Feel free to add as many as you need to paint your picture.

Dig and be creative. Take your time. Enjoy this process. There are no right or wrong answers—just objectives you want to accomplish.

You will also find additional value in this process by discussing these goals with others. Talk with your wife or husband, partner, good friends, close associates or even parents. The more time and thought that goes into this process, the clearer the picture can be.

Articulate the Goals

The very act of articulation begins the process of change in your business and your life, and makes your goals real. Secondly, it provides for input and alignment from appropriate team and/or family members.

With your picture of success coming to life, take that list of core values you worked on from the last chapter. How would your business look if you specifically begin to develop those values in and through your business? How could you be focused and intentional in developing those values? Here is another example of where a Success Factor Grid can help this process.

Spread your top 20 values out amongst the following brackets for your business in a SFG. Take each value and decide in which of the five business areas listed below that particular value is most needed, and plug it into the grid. Place your top five values in the top line in bold. These are the ones you want to focus on building, for obvious reasons.

1. Financial values
2. Product values

The Value Equation

3. Leadership values
4. Organizational health values
5. Reputation and legacy values

Here is an example of what your grid might look like:

Example Success Factor Grid: Long-Term Business Values Created

Financial	Products	Leadership	Organizational Health	Reputation
Abundance	Growth	Vision	Accessibility	Quality
Stability	Innovation	Boldness	Communication	Trust
Financial independence	Integrity	Stewardship	Clarity	Truth
Growing profit	Dependability	Effectiveness	Transparency	Fun

Now you have a nice simple tool that will allow you to begin building each of the above values specifically and intentionally in each area. Having this list ready and available will bring more clarity and focus as you work each day to find ways to implement these into your business. As you walk around your company, as you talk with your team members, as you chat with customers, keep these values in mind. Look for ways to bring one of these values into the conversation. Ask yourself, "How can I be more intentional with this value?"

Communicate

Good communication in many instances is difficult. It takes time and is not usually the strong suit of most entrepreneurs, but employee morale and productivity are only enhanced by communicating the *why*, the goals, and the strategic initiatives of your business. Your management team and your employees have a real desire

Painting a Picture of Success

to be excited about your business and the role they play in that success. They want to embrace your direction and purpose.

Create a poster of this chart and put it up in your business. Start every staff meeting with a short discussion around a certain value. Yes, this may seem silly, but people love these values. They want to work with a company where their values are more than just a slogan—where they are lived out daily. You will find that your employees will begin to emulate your steps. In turn, they will begin to live out their values, and especially those that correspond with yours. Imagine how that would change your company's culture and everyone's attitudes at work!

A Success Factor Grid can be used in many areas where you need to articulate specific goals or items that would define success—personal goals and aspirations, long-term business goals, departmental goals for the quarter, financial metrics, increases in manufacturing productivity, improved employee morale and health, sales improvement, meeting agendas, and even family vacations. There are many, many ways you can use this simple tool to increase the values you are developing.

Josh, one of our business partners, used a Success Factor Grid on a family vacation last summer. There were about 15 family members planning to spend a week together in a cabin in Minnesota, ages four to 40—you can see the train wreck coming . . . . So he sat everyone down and made a list of everything everyone wanted to do, and then they voted on the 10 must-do activities, i.e., their priorities for a successful vacation. Then Josh put together a plan to ensure that every day contained two of those 10 must-do events. The entire vacation went with little hassle. In fact, everyone said it was the best family get-together they had ever had. Success!

The Value Equation

Expand the Details

The chart below is an additional tool to help you look at different areas of work or business and, within each area, what specifically you would like to achieve, avoid, or preserve—three solid questions to ask in many areas. What specific goals do you want to achieve? What specific actions, behaviors, or mistakes do you want to avoid? What values, actions, goals, etc., do you want to preserve?

You can substitute other questions for specific areas of work or your business. What gives you the greatest feeling of joy, achievement, or satisfaction? What part of your job gives you the greatest pleasure? Where can you create the most impact, the most *value*?

Values to Achieve, Avoid, and Preserve

	Achieve	Avoid	Preserve
For my community	Products & services that serve the local community	The fear of saying yes	Opportunities for others
For my employees and coworkers	A work environment people love to be a part of	My strengths being overdone	Relationships that allow us to fail and pivot
For my family	Lasting memories	Kids testing my values and finding them false	Our sense of roots and stability
For my role	Work that uses my full potential	Perception that I don't deliver what I promise	Ownership of my schedule
For . . .	Business value that leads to referrals		

Ask your employees. What might you need to achieve or avoid or preserve in your management of them? Where would these three questions help in your business development efforts? Or in dealing with your best (or worst) customer? Or your banker, or your most important supplier? The options are unlimited.

We had a client who was in the semiconductor equipment business. They had decided the company needed to add a new line of innovative robotics to achieve a significant market differentiation and protect their older but significantly more profitable tools. It took two days of discussion to get the five senior managers to align on the key Success Factors (or strategic imperatives) to create success. But once this was achieved, they were able to move quickly because everyone was in agreement on the priorities and knew their roles and responsibilities—that is true alignment!

Why This Works

Study after study shows that your employees find significance and fulfillment doing a job that is meaningful—that makes a contribution to the creation of something important. It's not about the money, it is about *creating something of value,* yet they can only do this if you communicate your goals and values with them.

A Success Factor Grid produces clarity for the communication of goals and priorities to company employees and other stakeholders. This allows the team to focus on what is critical and align everyone to the fulfillment of that goal. Clarity and communication on where you are headed, and *why,* is a significant issue for most small businesses.

Several years ago, we had a client company that was led by an amazingly innovative and creative individual. However, he was a lousy communicator and strategically he was all over the map. Financially, his business was not doing well and his employees didn't understand where he was headed or what new and exciting business opportunity was next. We helped him develop a new and creative organizational structure that divided the company into several separate business units, each with specific products, services, employees, and focus. Then, we created a corporate development team to look

The Value Equation

at new business opportunities and develop specific plans for future growth. Suddenly, everyone had clarity—a focus on their role and purpose within the company.

This fairly simple change created significant value. Employee health and security, revenue per employee, gross profit, and net income increased dramatically. People were excited to come to work and the owner had a way to exercise his entrepreneurial skills without confusion and frustration. Success!

The Success Factor Grid can help you create simple yet profound and valuable transformation.

Summary

Being intentional about building your core values is transformational. Be creative. Look at the things you do and take advantage of every opportunity to build value. You will be amazed at the changes this simple act can bring to your business.

All change and future success start with a plan—a plan to create things of value. Innovation, growth, joy, legacy, quality, on-time delivery—*value*. None of these things can be achieved without an intentional, focused, and creative plan.

Start by looking at your long-term goals so the short-term goals lead to and are aligned with the long-term ones. Define what success looks like. What sounds fun and fulfilling? What are the various goals you want to achieve?

At Agora, we use the Success Factor Grid (SFG) to help clients and members of our workshops articulate and organize their thoughts and goals into a simple, coherent picture. We have given

Painting a Picture of Success

you a few examples of what some SFGs look like and how they may be used to create value. Success Factors Grids can be used to define success for a meeting, a fund-raising event, a large project, or even a family vacation. There are literally as many uses as your imagination can create.

For additional insight and examples of additional Success Factor Grids, please consult the Appendix or visit our website at AgoraConsulting.us.

4

ASSESSMENTS—
KNOWING WHERE YOU ARE

"We learned that a former prisoner of war had more to teach us about what it takes to find a path to greatness than most books on corporate strategy. Every good-to-great company embraced what we came to call the Stockdale Paradox: You must maintain unwavering faith that you can and will prevail in the end, regardless of the difficulties, AND at the same time have the discipline to confront the most brutal facts of your current reality, whatever they might be."

—Jim Collins, Good to Great

Jamie was the owner of a fairly successful custom cabinet shop. The business was hanging in there financially, but the employees were unhappy and there was a significant amount of employee turnover. Productivity was *terrible*—simply put, the business's employees did not really like Jamie. Yes, they respected him as the boss, but they resented his intrusion into the shop. Jamie had inherited the business from his uncle, and he did not know that much about

The Value Equation

woodworking. However, Jamie *thought* he knew quite a bit and was not bashful about sharing his opinion with the guys in the shop.

His view of what the shop employees thought of him was different from reality. He thought he was liked—after all, they laughed at his jokes—but he was not. He thought that the shop productivity was pretty good—it wasn't. He thought the employee turnover was standard practice, while in reality most cabinet shops have minimal turnover. Simply put, he was simply unaware of what others truly thought. He really thought he was where he wasn't. Together, we did a commercial personality assessment for him and he was surprised with the assessment results.

Fortunately, Jamie was all in. He took reality and ran with it. He worked hard on his leadership and management skills, improving where he was weak and gaining skills where he was strong. He even started taking weekly lessons on woodworking techniques—from his shop guys—that quickly became a lighthearted and enjoyable time.

What is your perception of your business? Of your abilities? What are others' perception of you and the business? Where is your business, really?

The third step in the Value Equation process assesses your current position, so you can plan for your success.

The Value Equation Process

Identify Core Values + Paint a Picture of Success + Assess Current Position + Create a Plan = SUCCESS

Assessments: Knowing Where You Are

Value Equation Step 3: Assessing Your Current Practices and Outcomes

Step 3 in the Value Equation process is assessment of your business from many angles—productivity, leadership, and communication, for starters. Periodically, clearly and honestly assessing your business is critical to creating significant value and business success. You need a thorough understanding of where you are before you begin to plan where you want to go. However, this part of the process can be quite involved and time consuming. When you look at all of the pieces to running a business—product development, retail sales, manufacturing and service operations, marketing, engineering, employee relations, finance, etc.—assessing all of these aspects in depth can get very complex.

While this is an important step in understanding exactly what you will need to do, many executives and business owners fail to take this step seriously. Perhaps they feel like they know their business better than anyone else? Yet, trying to create value and not exactly understanding the *why*, *where*, and *what* is like jumping in the car for a long trip and not looking at the gas gauge or a map.

This chapter is not meant to provide a vast array of assessment tools with a significant depth of evaluation. It is meant to encourage you to do periodic assessments with critical objectivity. Many excellent assessment tools have been published over the last several years. We have listed several of them in the Recommended Resources following this paragraph so you can dive as deep as you like. Please jump in—the more you learn, the better equipped you will be to create significant and lasting value.

The Value Equation

> **Recommended Resources**
> - DISC Personality and Leadership Profiles, see https://discprofile.com/what-is-disc/overview/
> - Bradberry, Travis, and Jean Greaves. *Emotional Intelligence 2.0*. Talent Smart, 2009. www.talentsmart.com
> - Buckingham, Marcus. *Stand Out 2.0 Assess Your Strengths, Find Your Edge, Win at Work*. One Thing Productions, Inc., 2015
> - All of the books mentioned in *The Value Equation* offer excellent assessment tools.
> - Agora Strategic Consulting offers significant, insightful, and valuable third-party business assessments.

For additional information, please visit our website at AgoraConsulting.us.

For the purposes of this book, we will look at two simple tools that will provide you with substantial insights into not only where you are, but where you need to go. We will look at a Values Assessment Scorecard and a similar scorecard for your business.

Values Assessment Scorecard

The Values Assessment Scorecard gives you the opportunity to gain clarity on how well you are delivering and living out your core values in and through your business. Where are you succeeding? Where do you need more focus and intentionality?

Assessments: Knowing Where You Are

Here is a partially completed Values Assessment Scorecard:

Example Values Assessment Scorecard

Top Values	Personal Score	Leadership Team Score	Key Employee Score	Key Advisor Score	Customer or Client Score
Financial					
Abundance	2.5	3	3	2.5	
Stability	2	3	3	2.5	
Financial Independence	1.5	1.5	1.5	1	
Growing profit	1.5	2	2	2	
Products					
Growth					2.5
Innovation					3
Integrity					3.5
Dependability					3
Leadership					
Vision					
Boldness					
Stewardship					
Effectiveness					
Organizational Health					
Accessibility					
Communication					
Clarity					
Transparency					
Reputation					
Quality					
Trust					
Truth					
Fun					

This tool contains the summary assessments from four critical groups of people within your company as well as your own input. While these assessments are fairly simple and straightforward, you will gain some interesting and perhaps challenging information.

The Value Equation

Does your business deliver dependable and innovative products? Are you, as a team leader, accessible? Are you trustworthy? Do you have fun? Simple but informative stuff.

Have each group place their scores on a separate sheet. First, place a score of 1 to 5 on how well you think your business is developing and living out your top 20 values in each box—1 being low and 5 being perfect. Take your time and be as objective as possible. It is human nature to be a bit hard on yourself and your business, but be fair and honest.

Second, have your management team rate your businesses value delivery. It will be interesting to see where their scores align with yours.

Third, have your key employees rate the same areas. Your employees are an important group as they add the true executable part of what you are trying to do. Alignment here is difficult and *fun*. Difficult to get the process started and fun when you start to see results. Actually, very fun when you see results!

Next, include your key advisors. Every business owner, executive, and manager needs a few advisors to help support and encourage his or her efforts—an accountability group and best friend rolled into one. Your accountant, banker, attorney, best customer, best friend, and your spouse or partner all make excellent advisors. Even if they don't know or understand the ins and outs of your business in depth, they can be of considerable help. Values are of universal appeal and understanding.

Finally, ask your customers or clients. They are the true recipients of your value delivery efforts. They are really the ones that count. An open, honest assessment from them can help create considerable value! Be careful here, however, because many times customers will

Assessments: Knowing Where You Are

give you an inflated, overly optimistic assessment. It is also a societal custom not to offend. Ask them to be real with you.

> **Let these values permeate your thoughts and business practices. More thought, more value created.**

We at Agora use the Values Assessment Scorecard for our own business, for a few key reasons. One, I as the leader need to know how I am doing in the creation and delivery of these critical values. The future success of my business depends on how well I and my team do here. Two, it keeps my top core values clearly in my mind. This may seem a bit silly, but I have found over many years of practice that having my goals clearly in my mind and thinking about them often produces significant dividends—like success! Assessing, thinking about them, and team discussions around them keeps them in play. The more I think, question, assess, and plan—the more these values are on my mind—and the more intentional and successful my delivery will be.

The third use for this scorecard is that it will also reveal where you are falling short and where your priorities are to deliver on your core values. This is an intentional process.

Collectively, these assessments should give you a fairly clear view of how you are doing in living and delivering on your core values. They will show what comes more naturally for you and your team as well as the areas where you will need more effort.

Think, be creative, take time, create success.

The Value Equation

Business Assessment Scorecard

Now, you need to look at your business in the same thoughtful, honest, and critical way. This assessment is more complicated and time consuming, but it yields great insight into your business operations and health.

Here are the areas and some of the questions that you need to ask and seek clarity around. Like the above Values Assessment Scorecard, there are many ways to look at this and literally thousands of questions to ask and types of information to seek. This is a simplified version that will show you something of the scope you can cover.

1. **Business position**
   - **Market:** How strong is the market you serve? Is it growing? Is it an old market or new, is it innovative, and does it serve a big market or a niche?
   - **Products and services:** Do your products and/or services create a market differentiation or do you compete on price? Is your pricing strategy driven by your values or is it reactive to customer "demands"?
   - **Credibility:** Do you deliver the best in class, or at a more standard set of criteria? Are you and your business trusted and seen as a person and organization with integrity?
   - **Revenue and business development:** Are you selling enough goods and services at a fair and reasonable profit? Do you have dedicated sales staff and resources?
   - **Competition:** Are you a market leader or follower? Who do you fear and why?

Assessments: Knowing Where You Are

2. **Customer Satisfaction**
   - **Customer satisfaction:** Do you deliver "wow," or just "me too"? Are your customers loyal and not concerned about price?
   - **Product delivery:** Are your deliveries on time? How often do you make excuses for late delivery?
   - **Product quality:** Is your product quality outstanding or reasonable, or poor? Is your service delivery met with a smile or grudging acceptance?

3. **Leadership and Management**
   - **Vision:** Do you have a clear vision and goals for the future? Is everyone on your team on board with the company goals?
   - **Leadership:** Do you challenge, hold employees accountable, preach or teach, and embrace your values?
   - **Communication of vision:** Does everyone in your business (employees, customers, suppliers, etc.) understand and embrace your vision and goals for the company?
   - **Clarity of internal communication:** How do members of your team or your employees communicate with each other? Where and how does trust play a role in company communication?
   - **Strength of management team:** Do you have a team or a bunch of individuals?
   - **Accountability:** Do you and your team hold each other accountable? How do you enforce good behavior and counter bad behavior?

The Value Equation

- **Overall employee health:** Do your employees enjoy their roles and embrace the company values? Is your office, store, or factory organized and healthy?

4. **Business Planning**
    - **Business planning:** Do you have a clear, creative, realistic plan in place? Are you more proactive or reactive?
    - **Financial planning:** Do you proactively manage your cash flow, or does it manage you? Do you know your key financial metrics and why these are important?

5. **Product Development, Production, and Quality**
    - **Shop planning and organization:** Is there a process for scheduling your "production" cycle of products or services?
    - **Shop management:** Do your shop and service supervisors provide quality communication to their employees regarding company policies, procedures, and status?
    - **Shop quality and delivery:** Do you know the shop/service center delivery or production status?
    - **Tools, equipment, and facilities:** Do you know if your tools, equipment, and facilities are outdated? Do you subscribe to trade journals and attend trade shows to look for the latest and best practices?

6. **Financial Position and Health**
    - **Financial strength:** Have you engaged in short-term and long-term financial planning? Do you trust your internal financial statements?
    - **Gross profit margin:** Do you routinely calculate gross profit margins for your business? Are these gross mar-

Assessments: Knowing Where You Are

gins broken down by product lines to determine product winners and losers?

- **Net income:** Is your net income sufficient to sustain the company through market and sales fluctuations?

- **Cash and working capital:** Do you have cash-flow projections? Are future cash flows adequate to ensure critical payments (payroll, accounts payable, debt payments, etc.)?

- **Assets:** Are your business assets adequate for continued operations? Are your fixed and long-term assets (buildings and major equipment) hiding potential liabilities such as mandatory upgrades or repairs?

- **Liabilities and debt:** Do you know all your company liabilities (potential refunds, returns, legal actions, taxes, etc.)? Is your debt serviceable through anticipated revenues?

7. **Future Growth and Direction**

    - **Growth potential:** Do you have a good feel for the market and where your business growth potential is?

    - **Capital required:** Are future capital requirements identified due to aging equipment, plants, or facilities? Do your sales forecasts incorporate future capital requirements for expanding plant operations?

    - **Return on investment potential:** Are you able to calculate your project, service, or product return on investment potential?

We have developed a Business Assessment Scorecard form that you can download to use for this assessment. While the example here and on the website is based on a manufacturing company, you

The Value Equation

can easily adapt it to retail, software, service, etc. companies. Find it at AgoraConsulting.us.

Like the Values Assessment Scorecard, place a rating on a scale of 1 to 5 (1 for very poor and 5 for outstanding) for how well you are doing *currently* in creating and delivering that particular capability or procedure in your business. I have chosen to use a simple 1 to 5 rating system. You can also use the old "traffic light" (red/low score, yellow/midrange score, and green/high score) color coding for visibility. Feel free to use a different method if you prefer.

The most important aspect of this assessment is *objectivity*. Ask other members of your team to help you in your assessment. Your management team is obvious, but have your accounting and finance team, shop employees, retail staff, software team, etc., comment and assess.

For example, look at the first assessment area, the one that focuses on your business operations and market position. How would you (and others) rate your business market position and competition, credibility, your future product development, etc.? These are the values that others will initially see and use to evaluate your business. Are these areas either a strength or weakness? Refer to the assessment questions listed above and be as objective as possible.

The Business Assessment Scorecard shows you clearly where you need to prioritize your efforts in aligning your business practices to your core values. Obviously, areas and functions with low scores are in need of major focus for improvement. Middle ratings are not as critical, but will obviously need corrective measures. However, you also want to create additional value in top-scoring areas. Making adjustments and improvements in each of these areas, while focus-

Assessments: Knowing Where You Are

ing on your Key Growth Factors (more on these below), will help you to create focused and intentional transformation.

Your ability to truly assess and think critically about your business on an ongoing basis is one of the most important abilities you can possess as a business leader. Henry Cloud calls it "integrity,"[1] and Jim Collins calls it "confronting the brutal facts."[2] James Kouzes and Barry Posner describe it as "challenging the process."[3] These are some of the best business thinkers and advisors today. It is a truly clear, honest, and insightful assessment that you want. You want and need your business to have integrity and be whole and structurally sound. The insights you gain here, in this part of the Value Equation process, will pay large dividends in the future.

One final word on assessment. Your business is a living organization. Things change *constantly*. Therefore, you need to do periodic assessments on your business to continue to build value and deliver success. I would recommend quarterly, critical business assessments. This will allow you to see progress while not getting out of alignment. At Agora, we do quarterly business reviews (assessments) and benefit greatly from them. Do the hard work, be honest and real, and understand that true transformation doesn't happen overnight.

Summary

It is critical, as a business owner or executive, that you understand exactly where your business is. A clear and honest assessment of your business is critical to creating significant value and business success. You need to know where you are before you begin to plan where you want to go. In this chapter, we introduce two assessment tools to help you understand your current status.

The Value Equation

One, the Values Assessment Scorecard, gives you an opportunity to understand how well you are currently living your top core values.

Two, the Business Assessment Scorecard, gives you and other team members an opportunity to assess your current business practices and results.

These tools give you critical data on where exactly you need to put your focus and intentional efforts to create short- and long-term value.

For additional insight and examples of how we use both the Values Assessment Scorecard and the Business Assessment Scorecard, as well as additional assessment materials and tools, please visit our website at AgoraConsulting.us.

Notes

1. Cloud, Henry. *Integrity: The Courage to Meet the Demands of Reality.* HarperBusiness, 2006.
2. Collins, James. *Good to Great: Why Some Companies Make the Leap and Others Don't.* HarperBusiness, 2001.
3. Kouzes, James and Barry Posner. *The Leadership Challenge: How to Make Extraordinary Things Happen in Organizations.* Jossey-Bass; 6th edition, April 2017.

5

IDENTIFYING CRITICAL KEYS TO GROWTH

"Research confirms that organizations with a strong corporate culture based on a foundation of shared values outperformed other firms by a huge margin."

—James Kouzes and Barry Posner, *The Leadership Challenge*

Ian's new plan for his company was to communicate his values and what his company stood for to his customers—with marketing that was targeted to his customers, but not about specific products. This message revealed what was important to Ian's company and the history of how he got started—to explain his passion, his *why*.

Ian's products weren't outdated, but the company's image was. It was becoming clear that one of the main reasons for his company's revenue slump was a failure to adapt to the new ways of connecting with customers. Word of mouth wasn't going to sustain his company. One of his longer-term goals was to introduce new products, but new products alone would not have turned the tide for him—his company

The Value Equation

lacked character and vision, in the eyes of his customers, and that's what we helped him focus his efforts on in the first 100 days.

Ian understood he couldn't stand still and watch the world change around him. He acted. The first step was to get his management team and employees onboard with the changes. It was hard at first, but then he explained why he wanted the changes. He explained he wanted to stand for something that was good. Once his team truly understood what he wanted to do and why, they were in sync.

Then he had to get buy-in from his customers. He did this through website updates that clearly demonstrated his quality product lines and communicated his company values to his customers and community. He coordinated a social media campaign that targeted a network for his quality products (with reasonable prices) that resonated with his specific customer base. His plan was to make believers of his customers as well as his employees.

Once his new marketing campaign was established and had connected customers, Ian was able to show customers and employees why he was in business. As he moved to the next stage, he started introducing new products that demonstrated his values of honest quality and dependability. His revenue started trending upward and the situation for Ian began to ease.

Ian's fear began to fade, and he started to truly enjoy the steady growth he was witnessing. His employees started to see a change as well. They were no longer spending time researching cheaper parts or new places to sell his products—his customers were coming to him effortlessly because they liked his values. He started thinking about developing a "next gen" product unlike anything he'd done before—which was what he truly loved to do and was the reason he went into business: He loved making those things he was always looking for but could never find.

Identifying Critical Keys to Growth

Like Ian, if you've painted the picture of your success and assessed your current status, you're ready for the next step in the Value Equation process: the business plan. Having a plan that provides a clear focus and allows appropriate staff buy-in allows your business plan to flow and create success.

We are not talking about the old, traditional business plan with its narrative and fluffy stuff. And we certainly aren't talking about bland and meaningless mission statements. We need *specifics* and *clarity*. Something short, simple, and to the point.

We use a way of business planning that is simple, yet dynamic in its effect. One of the reasons many business owners fail to plan is because traditional business planning is methodical, time consuming, and, well . . . really boring. The busier you get, the harder it is to take time to plan, and no one likes boring. But plan you must, to achieve your new goals. So, let me introduce you to an Agora concept and tool called *Key Growth Factors*.

Value Equation Step 4: Defining Your Key Growth Factors to Develop Your Plan

The fourth step in the Value Equation process is defining your Key Growth Factors. These are the basis for your plan to create success.

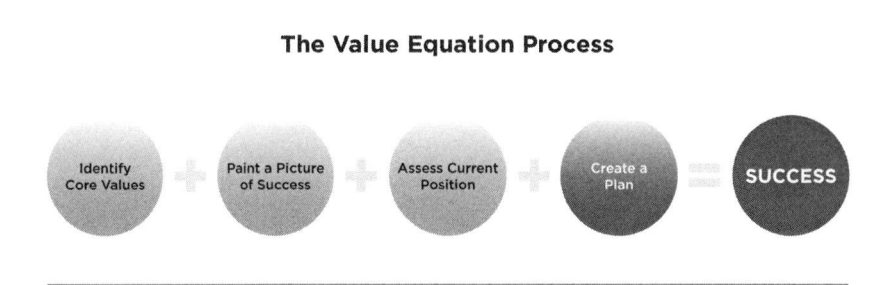

The Value Equation Process

Identify Core Values + Paint a Picture of Success + Assess Current Position + Create a Plan = SUCCESS

The Value Equation

If you have been tracking with us, you have done several things as you learned how to apply the Value Equation process.

1. You *defined* your top core values.
2. You *painted* a picture of what would define success—of what success would look like for you and your business.
3. You *articulated* your picture into one, or several, Success Factor Grids.
4. You *assessed* your business—its strengths, weaknesses, people, systems, operations, etc., the creation of value through your business, and your progress toward the fulfillment of your Success Factors. And you understand that you need to regularly *reassess* your business to adapt to changing conditions.

Throughout this process, you will have noticed several things, good and bad, that have and could have a dramatic effect on the creation of value in your business and your life. It could be your business's sales strategy, your operational problems, your lack of working capital, productivity issues, or just the lack of fun. What will jump out at you are the significant things that could have an incredible impact on your business—just the few key items that are your true priorities.

Remember the old 80/20 rule? We are looking for the 20 percent—the key, critical things that could have an 80 percent effect on the value produced by your business. Those few things, if you focus on them and make significant improvement, could have a huge, transformational impact. At Agora, we call these Key Growth Factors.

Identifying Critical Keys to Growth

Key Growth Factors

In our experience in working with hundreds of companies, Key Growth Factors are usually related to the following areas:

1. Your leadership and management style
2. The communication of your vision, purpose, and goals
3. Business development, sales, and revenue
4. Productivity and gross profit margin improvements
5. Employee, vendor, and customer communication
6. Employee morale and organizational health
7. Most importantly, the ability to align the above to your core values

We want the emphasis to be on determining what factors need to be changed to make a key or significant change *in a positive way*. Note the phrase—in a positive way. Simply changing a negative practice to a more positive practice does not necessarily create a positive result. Fixing a business practice without fixing the true cause is usually not productive or successful. Therefore, we want to find the Key Growth Factors and then develop proactive and positive plans and practices that provide significant business transformation, growth, and success.

If you have done a thorough, detailed, and honest business assessment, you will uncover many candidates for your Key Growth Factors. You can't miss them. Yes, you will have to be creative in developing solutions to improving those issues—but simply identifying the primary items and issues that need to be adjusted is much of the work here.

The Value Equation

Remember Brad, who installed cameras in the shop? His Key Growth Factors were around sales. As in many companies, a big improvement in revenue would produce a big improvement in many other areas. In his fear that the company would fail, Brad was too focused on responding to RFQs (requests for quotes). He kept his team and shop functioning fairly well, yet the result was a lot of low-margin business. If he could change his approach and gain additional higher-margin business, it would have a dramatic effect.

We helped him create a new business development strategy that did in fact create significant growth and resulted in great improvement in his company's financial health. His business grew its revenue by 26 percent the first year after the execution of the new strategy and doubled his profit margin. This Key Growth Factor created huge value. And guess what—as the revenue grew, Brad's fear died away!

And Karen? Her Key Growth Factors were to focus on teaching while minimizing the hassles and time of purchasing, manufacturing, sales, employee management, accounting, etc., of her quilting business. There was major synergy between the teaching of techniques to make quilting easier, faster, and more fun, and the selling of the tools that made those techniques possible. However, she was really unhappy doing the "business" stuff, so we needed to help her find a solution to this problem.

We worked with Karen to help her identify her critical core values and goals and develop a plan—and well, we sort of blew up her business.

We divided her business into three segments:

1. A seminar and teaching group

Identifying Critical Keys to Growth

2. An innovative product development group

3. A product manufacturing and sales group.

Then we sold her manufacturing/sales segment to a successful hobby company for a royalty income stream and formed a new product development joint venture with the same hobby company, which allowed Karen fun creativity toward developing new products and a nice royalty—with no "business" issues to worry about.

Fulfilled and happy, Karen retained the teaching company and now teaches, produces videos, and gives seminars (even on Mediterranean cruises). Nice transformation!

You need to determine what your Key Growth Factors are and spend whatever time and effort and money as necessary to understand them and develop your plan. On these few things, you can build significant success. Identifying these key factors is critical. This is the road to the transformation of your business.

Value Equation Step 4: The 100-Day Plan

At this point in the Value Equation process, you need to pull everything together into a plan. An articulated, clear, easy-to-communicate plan. However, rather than write a complex 60-page document that will be completely obsolete by the time it is finished, we have developed a simpler solution—the *100-Day Plan*. We have chosen to focus on just 100 days. Too often, business owners create larger, more complicated plans and get bogged down and fail. It seems like a good idea, but the task is just too daunting. Start with 100 days—three months. Simple, focused, intentional. Begin to take action. Jim Collins, in his excellent book *Good to Great,*[1] talks

The Value Equation

about a "heavy flywheel"—and your task is to get the flywheel rotating as fast as possible.

If you know anything about flywheels, you know that they take a huge amount of energy to get up to speed. If you are persistent, it will begin to move. Continue the effort and the flywheel will move faster and faster—and it will become easier and easier to keep it in motion.

The point here is to focus on your first 100 days. Just get started.

Collins says, "Good to great comes about by a cumulative process—step by step, action by action, decision by decision, turn by turn of the flywheel—that adds up to sustained and spectacular results."[2]

Let me walk you through the process.

First, the 100-Day Plan can be laid out as a four-column grid. Simple. Second, if you have been working through the Value Equation process with us to this point, you *already have* two of the four components for the columns.

The first column will contain your initial Key Growth Factors—those few items that will produce big change. The second column will contain a summary of the actions you will be taking to meet your Key Growth Factor objectives. Each of these two items will be discussed below.

The third column will contain your business goals from your long-term Picture of Success as defined by your long-term Success Factor Grid. List each of your Success Factors in the third column, labeled Long-Term Success Factors in the example below. The fourth

Identifying Critical Keys to Growth

column will contain your top core values as you determined from the second core values exercise you performed early in the book.

Here is a simple example:

Example 100-Day Plan

Key Growth Factors and Priority	100-Day Action Plan	Long-Term Success Factors	Core Values
1. Improve Sales		$10M in Revenue	Abundance Growth

Here is the concept of how to use and create an action plan for the next 100 days from this tool.

List your Key Growth Factors in the first column, by priority. Given the issues and business practices that need to change to create success, a priority list will shake itself out. Some items will be of significant priority, some less so. Take some time to prioritize these.

Now look at your long-term Success Factors. The process here is to align the priorities of your Key Growth Factors in the left column to the execution and creation of value as represented by your long-term Success Factors (goals) in the third column. What you are trying to do is create sustainable success as defined by those Success Factors. That is specifically the value you want to create.

If you want to create sustainable success, you need to fulfill your longer-term success factors. If you simply decided on a plan to meet some of your Key Growth Factors in and of themselves, you might

The Value Equation

be solving problems and creating value—but not necessarily long-term *sustainable* value.

Therefore, you need to prioritize and align your Key Growth Factors to your longer-term success factors. In the example, the number one priority is to improve sales. This is a very common problem with most businesses. This Key Growth Factor would then be in alignment with the long-term goal of reaching $10M in revenue.

Note that by the time you reach this point in your planning, you may want or need to change your long-term Success Factors. As you go through the Value Equation process, you will become more observant and will learn much about your business. This is one of the significant aspects of the process. The more you observe, the more you learn, and the more value you will be able to create. That said, you may also want to change your priorities or long-term goals as a result. That's perfect. Make the changes and realign as necessary. Keep the end goal and your core values in mind.

Next, place your core values in the final column. Again, the concept of this tool is to reach alignment of your Key Growth Factors and action plans with both your long-term Success Factors *and* your core values. This is key! We have placed the core values of *abundance* and *growth* in the last column of the example. These are two core values that could be achieved by reaching our success factor of $10M in revenue.

Lastly, we need to focus on developing an *action plan* to achieve your identified Success Factors—determine the changes necessary and the actions required in the next 100 days.

Identifying the real issues and the 20 percent of effort that can create significant value is huge—and once you've done that, you need to *execute* on those goals. Don't think about big changes; take

Identifying Critical Keys to Growth

small steps and zero in on the critical components of each goal. Work on executing the basics, the "blocking and tackling" of your business, first. What can you do over the next 100 days to begin the transformation process? You won't likely achieve all of your long-term Success Factors in this 100 days, but you'll start your business moving in that direction. Think micro-steps rather than big leaps. Think of your business as a flywheel that you must get moving—slowly building momentum . . . to *success*.

Example Step Development: Increasing Revenue

Let's look at one example of developing a specific action plan: increasing revenue. Many small- to midsized businesses struggle with revenue. It is the single most important element of any business. At Agora, I half-jokingly say, "The three most important elements of any business are revenue, revenue, and revenue!" There are ways you can fight that battle and grow your business. There are many fine books and materials available that offer strategies to increase sales and revenue. You might consider studying some of these if you struggle with this, but here are some suggestions that may get you started.

Action plan example: improving sales and revenue.

1. Conduct customer interviews: What do customers think of your products and services, pricing, and quality? What is most important to them? What else do they need—what additional products and services might they like you to provide? Significant time here is important. Your customers can give you key information that can help you provide valuable new products and services. The deeper you go with your customers the more value they will provide.

The Value Equation

2. Evaluate your market: Are there potential customers you are not serving? Are you serving the correct customers? Where else might you go to find new customers? (For instance, a building material supplier might try and work directly with the developer and eliminate the pricing pressure from the contractor.)

3. Read, study, and implement a Blue Ocean strategy—an innovative and insightful business development strategy developed by W. Chan Kim and Renee Mauborgne and described in their book **Blue Ocean Strategy**.[3]

4. Price increase strategy: Is there a possibility that by increasing your product capability, quality, delivery speed, etc., you could increase your price . . . and your gross margin?

5. Team brainstorming: Gather the team together and critique/evaluate your products and services. Ask them to brainstorm ideas, potential customers, new ideas, etc.

While we understand that developing a successful sales strategy can be complicated, these ideas will get you started with some proven tactics. Also, we have found that the Blue Ocean strategy concept is one of the best tools for achieving sales growth and has produced substantial results for many of our clients.

> What is a Blue Ocean strategy? In this bestselling book, *Blue Ocean Strategy*, the authors, W. Chan Kim and Renée Mauborgne, describe how to make the competition irrelevant by creating your own "blue ocean," an untapped, new market that is wide open for growth.

Identifying Critical Keys to Growth

The final step in creating your 100-Day Plan is to list the actions needed to achieve your Key Growth Factors in the second column. Here is a simple example:

100-Day Plan: Action Column Complete

Key Growth Factors and Priority	100-Day Action Plan	Long-Term Success Factors	Core Values
1. Improve sales	• Blue Ocean strategy • Customer interviews • Team brainstorming	$10M in revenue	Abundance Growth
2. Improve organization and communication	• Publish vision statement • Implement management team monthly assessment and communication meeting	40 loyal and happy employees	Communication Vision Clarity Truth
3. Equip all employees with all the tools they need to succeed	• Conduct employee and management interviews to assess needs	40 loyal and happy employees	Accessibility Trust Boldness Stewardship Effectiveness
4. Focus on creating additional gross profit margin to increase cash	• Perform detailed operations assessment to find Key Growth Factors • Create plan (SFG) for operations	$10M in revenue with 15% net profit	Stability Growing profit Financial freedom
5. Improve product quality and delivery	• Hire QA manager • Implement QA plan	Known as "*the* place to buy"	Quality Innovation Integrity Dependability

The 100-Day Plan creates a huge benefit to you and your business. It shows you how to *align* your business actions and plans with your Key Growth Factors, your longer-term Success Factors, and your core values. In the example, by improving sales we move towards achieving not only the SFG of $10M in revenue, but also the core values of growth and abundance. By improving organizational communication, we not only help achieve the goal of having 40 loyal employees, but also the values of vision, clarity, and truth. Remember, ultimately you are trying to achieve your long-term Success Factors and your core values.

The Value Equation

The 100-Day Plan does not need to be complicated to be effective. The goal is to keep it simple—focused and intentional. Get your flywheel moving!

Value Equation Step 5: Review, Assess, Adjust, and Keep Going

Life changes, business changes, and the market changes. Therefore, you need to periodically review where you are and how your business is progressing toward the successful accomplishment of your plan. As you execute your action plan, you will continue to observe and assess your business. You will see and learn a lot.

We recommend that you do a periodic review of your business to assess where things are and adjust your plan accordingly. As you accomplish goals, your priorities may need to change. As people step up, as communication improves, and as markets change, many goals might be achieved sooner than expected. Stop and assess and adjust as necessary.

Many of our clients hold a monthly business review meeting with their key management personnel. They do a department-by-department and financial review of their business. This needs to be an open, honest discussion to maximize the value of the review. You can do this, even if you have a small business with limited management. Pick a team of your best employees and get their input. Meet with your wife or husband, best friend, accountant. The point is you need to do a periodic assessment and make sure you are making progress. Identify any needed adjustments and work them into your plan. It is always better to ask multiple individuals to provide you with feedback.

Identifying Critical Keys to Growth

In truth, the process is never over. Successful companies and organizations continually rework the process—through formal or informal periodic, internal process reviews, strategic planning, or cultural processes. The challenge in adapting to a changing marketplace is to continuously validate the core values and success factors that enable success for you and your business.

So—review, assess, make changes as necessary, and then keep going. Build those micro-steps into your 100-Day Plan to create value and success.

Summary

The Value Equation process is a simple yet powerful tool to help you develop, articulate, assess, and align your business goals and objectives to create significant value—in your business and in your life.

First, you need to *identify the values* that are important to you—for your personal life and for your business.

Second, you need to *paint a picture* of what success looks like for you. Your greatest passions and desires, the dreams for your business, and your defining aspirations should all be included. This gives you direction and purpose, and something to live for.

Then, *articulate* those goals and your core values into a *Success Factor Grid*. This is a specific list of key items that define success. It gives you a specific checklist—a clear, specific vision of what is desired, required, and critical to achieve success. Success Factor Grids can be simple or complex. They may be multifaceted to include many elements of your business. Success Factor Grids can also be used to define success for almost any activity—company goals, meeting goals, production activities, financial goals, personal health goals, even family vacations. Ask and answer the question, "What does success look like?"

Third, *assess* the current state of your business and how well you are living out and creating your core values, to understand where you have strengths and weaknesses, problems, issues, etc. This will allow you to develop a plan to achieve success. The more honest and real you are during these assessments, the better your chances are of achieving the transformation you desire.

Fourth, based on your assessment, *develop* your *Key Growth Factors*—a prioritized list of those few elements that will produce significant value. This is the old 80/20 rule—the 20 percent of change needed to produce 80 percent of the value.

The *100-Day Plan* brings all of these elements into a simple plan of action that is focused on achieving your Key Growth Factors and, ultimately, your long-term Success Factors and core values. We use 100 days as a short-term time frame to allow you to focus on the immediate priorities and begin to build momentum—significant change and near-term growth that is the foundation for your transformation.

Lastly, we build in a periodic *business review* to *reassess* and adjust so that you maintain your course toward building fun and exciting value and fulfillment. This is essentially an ongoing process that you started as you developed your plan and is critical to adapting to changing conditions—to achieve *and* sustain your success.

Align your core values, transform your business, and create sustainable success!

Identifying Critical Keys to Growth

You will find more examples of each of the above Value Equation processes and tools on our website at AgoraConsulting.us.

Notes

1. Collins, James. *Good to Great: Why Some Companies Make the Leap and Others Don't.* HarperBusiness, 2001.
2. Ibid., p. 165.
3. Kim, W. Chan and Renée Mauborgne. *Blue Ocean Strategy: How to Create Uncontested Market Space and Make the Competition Irrelevant.* Harvard Business Review Press, Expanded Edition, 2015.

6
VALUE-ALIGNED LEADERSHIP

"After two decades of working with CEOs and their teams of senior executives, I've become absolutely convinced that the seminal difference between successful companies and mediocre or unsuccessful ones has little, if anything, to do with what they know or how smart they are; it has everything to do with how healthy they are."

—Patrick Lencioni, *The Advantage*

Years ago, I witnessed one of the worst examples of leadership I have ever seen during an airshow at a West Coast naval air station. An older lieutenant was in charge of safety on the ramp and needed to position his enlisted troops between the crowd and the taxiways to maintain a safe separation from the taxiing aircraft. Rather than communicate to his troops the task and its goal, he walked the group down the flight line, pointed to each one and said, "Stand here." No communication, no trust, and no responsibility. Arrogant and very

The Value Equation

unproductive. Rather than take five minutes to explain, he took a half hour to position everyone himself.

Great leadership is not the sole domain of corporate boardrooms and government halls. It is found everywhere. Perhaps some have worldwide influence and others influence just a few. Great leadership makes the difference between creating a little value and creating significant and lasting value, whether in business, nonprofit organizations, or in government.

Remember, it's about building value, and you can't do it alone!

Over the years, I have observed many examples and made notes on great leadership skills. The following guidelines sum up many critical practices on how best to lead an organization and will maximize the creation of value in your company. The skills and recommendations below can truly transform your business. It is all about living a life aligned with your values.

Value-Aligned Leadership Competencies

1. It's not about you
2. Start with *why*
3. Communicate with clarity
4. Develop great people
5. Focus on creating value, constantly
6. Know the truth
7. Seek rest

Competency #1: It's Not About You

No, it is *really* not. It's not about you . . . it is about *them*—your employees, your customers, your vendors, your employees' families,

Value-Aligned Leadership

your family, your stakeholders. Success in business is about creating value through and from people . . . them. You can't do it alone. You need them.

In our consulting practice, workshops, speaking engagements, in fact in all that we do, we hit this pretty hard. There is an age-old term for this that we use called *servant leadership*.

Servant leadership is about equipping your employees with the tools, training, procedures, and equipment they need to succeed. If they succeed, then guess what—*you* succeed. And if you care for them, truly care, if you put them first, if you show them value and respect, if you give them meaningful jobs and the freedom to do their jobs—they will love you. Truly!

Employee productivity and retention is built on trust and believing that the boss cares. It is about creating a great place to work—a place where they are respected, trusted, empowered, and inspired.

> There is a successful company in northern Colorado where the leadership of the company truly lives out servant leadership. Because the leaders care, their employees and customers and vendors care. The business does not run a swing shift or work weekends, even when demand is high, because it is bad for the employees and their families. They pay their bills on time because it is good for the vendor—and a successful vendor is good for business. The average employee has been with the company for over *11 years*. Imagine the cost saving and productivity value created with so little turnover.

The Value Equation

Many of the great leaders throughout history have been servant leaders—loved and inspired by their people. George Washington, Abraham Lincoln, Robert E. Lee, Martin Luther King, Mother Teresa, and Billy Graham. Humility, putting others first, faith, trust—servant leadership. It's not about you, it's about them!

Competency #2: Start with *Why*

Every business owner can explain what they do and how they do it, but not many can explain *why* they do what they do. Great leaders can and are able to inspire people to act. "Those who are able to inspire give people a sense of purpose or belonging," says Simon Sinek, in his book *Start with Why*. "Those who are inspired are willing to pay a premium or endure inconvenience, even personal suffering."

Martin Luther King had a dream shared by many, and they loved and followed him. He inspired. George Washington inspired. Mother Teresa inspired. They still do!

People love to be inspired, they love to be part of a movement. They are attracted to the why. Tom's gives away shoes, Oboz plants trees, Patagonia gives one percent of its profit to environmental organizations, but it goes deeper than that. It is also the values that those companies practice, that their key leaders live out daily.

When people understand your *why*, the reason you do things, the core values you believe in and live every day, they will be attracted to that—your *why*. If you really believe in innovation and live that value, then you will attract others who value innovation. Being first, being a leader in a market, having a no-questions-asked return policy or a standard of no defects, treating employees with respect and trust. These are qualities, values that employees, customers, and vendors will be inspired by.

Can people be inspired while working for an insurance agent? How about a steel company? A gardener? Of course! But you must know your *why*, you must know your core values. You must communicate and live those values—daily, in alignment with your business management, goals and objectives.

Competency #3: Communicate

Time is your most precious commodity. As things get busy, as the fires build, as pressures mount, the value that falls through the cracks is communication. But lack of communication has significant consequences.

It is impossible for the people in a company to build much value or success if you are not communicating with your employees or your team. *Impossible.* Communication is a critical skill for getting your employees and team up, moving, and creating value—yet many leaders struggle with this. About 70 percent of the clients we work with are assessed by us as having poor company and interpersonal communication.

What are the symptoms? Confusion, poor company morale, lack of trust, inefficiencies, cost overruns, mistakes, fear, and meeting after meeting. The biggest indicator is the death of your time—killed by people asking the little, seemingly inconsequential questions. "Where is that?" "What did he say?" "Has that been approved?" They ask questions they should know the answers to—that they *do* know the answers to—but have been blindsided too many

The Value Equation

times by a lack of communication. Rather than take the initiative and possibly be embarrassed, they punt and ask you.

Simple things, when not done in alignment to company values, wind up undermining the direction of employees and actually move the company backwards . . . little by little. A lack of communication about important goals, whether short-term or long-term, creates wasted effort when employees have to realize they don't know the *what* or the *how* of their next task, and have to circle back around to ask.

However, when things are effectively and clearly communicated, when people understand where the company is headed, understand their roles and responsibilities, and understand the desired outcomes, then significant value is created. We have seen amazing results materialize when clear and effective communication happens.

Know and Communicate Your Success Factors

Your list of Success Factors (developed from the Success Factor Grid, earlier) is a great communication tool. Once everyone is clear about your Success Factors for the company and how these Success Factors align with company values and goals, they become clarifying, cohesive, and aligning functions. So, make them simple, straightforward and clear. It is hard to embrace something that isn't clear.

Communicate with Clarity

In *The Advantage* by Patrick Lencioni,[1] clarity makes up three of the four disciplines he recommends to achieve organizational health. "Communicate to employees," says Mr. Lencioni, "clearly, repeatedly, enthusiastically, and repeatedly [that's not a typo].

Value-Aligned Leadership

When it comes to reinforcing clarity, there is no such thing as too much communication."[2]

Confusion is the hallmark of a dysfunctional company. Clarity is the foundation—especially clarity of company values and the success factors of a successful business. Clarity means that the message has not only been communicated by you but that it has also been *understood* by the recipient. Clarity requires thought, articulation, patience, and often, repeated conversations—which take time.

How do you know when you are achieving clarity? One indicator is when those little, seemingly inconsequential questions begin to disappear. Another powerful indicator is when employees take actions that support Success Factors before management intervenes and directs them to action. What a dynamic organization . . . instead of micromanaging employees, your time is spent directing the future of the company!

Competency #4: Develop Great People

A business creates and delivers value through its people—at all levels of the organization. If your employees are confused, angry, not getting along, and not aligned to your business values, then you will not have much success. Great companies have great people! Therefore, developing great people needs to be a major priority. Here are a few ideas to learn from.

One: Create a Cohesive Leadership Team

Remember that old story about everyone in the rowboat rowing in the same direction?

In 2002, the CEO of a company that I worked for (this was pre-Agora days) in Silicon Valley came to our executive team with

The Value Equation

an innovative idea. He decided that he wanted to create a new business unit to broaden our market scope. My job was to purchase the businesses that would make up this new unit. The CEO's original thought was that the rest of the team would execute the new business. The problem was no one on the team wanted to have anything to do with this concept. It was an interesting idea and perhaps a good one, but everybody on the team—except our CEO—thought it did not fit our business model and market. End of story, right? No.

The CEO was so impressed with the idea that he informed his executives: "I'll run the business unit myself,"—and unfortunately that is exactly what he did. Or at least he tried to. Although the business was eventually purchased, it never made money. No one else ever stepped up and supported the concept. No R&D, no engineering, no sales or manufacturing support . . . he was on his own. It was an unmitigated disaster from day one. After a year of frustration on all sides (including the CEO), the business was sold back to the seller we bought the business from for $1. No joke.

Team cohesion exists when everyone on the team not only understands the mission, but also embraces the mission. Team cohesion exists when everyone on the team not only understands their roles and responsibilities, but embraces them. Communication, clarity, trust, understanding, and buy-in all help develop team cohesion. But don't forget your *why*. The more your team is inspired by the mission and why you are doing what you are doing, the better the buy-in and teamwork.

Two: Make Employee Success a Priority

Underlying the critical competencies of "It's not about you" and "Develop a cohesive team" is a fundamental truth about building

Value-Aligned Leadership

leadership and successful teams. You have to focus on making the employees successful so that your company (and eventually you) will also become successful. If your employees continue to fail, then the chances of the company's sustainable success are dim. Seems pretty straightforward.

Donald Rumsfeld once said, "You go to war with the army you have, not the army you might want or wish to have at a later time." We must make do with what we have. And sometimes, *we* are the problem, not them.

How many times have you heard it said that good employees are hard to find? Some entrepreneurs and owners of small businesses complain about this, but others do not. Most satisfied employees value a challenging and exciting job and the culture of their workplace above the importance of wages. It is not the money that makes most employees happy, it is the enjoyment of their environment. This will only become more important as millennials and subsequent generations enter the work force.

Make your employees' jobs valuable and meaningful. Start by including them in decisions that affect their work life. Give them jobs that have an opportunity to create value. This is the single most important component to an enjoyable work environment. Everyone wants jobs that are meaningful.

Three: Make Sure Your Employees Have All the Tools They Need for Success

This includes appropriate computers and IT systems, appropriate training, a clean, safe, and productive work environment, appropriate supervision and support, an organizational structure and management that is supportive yet holds everyone accountable, and

The Value Equation

a culture that supports a work-hard, play-hard attitude. This also includes your time as leader. The goal is to engage and manage them . . . starting with your commitment and clarity to their role in fulfilling the Success Factors and aligning their jobs to company values.

Four: Create Something Bigger Than Yourself

Create a mission-focused mindset, something that is bigger and more important than yourself and your employees. Something that will actually make a difference. It could be hosting an annual fundraiser, hosting a special-needs formal, everyone being a big-brother or big-sister, or sponsoring an immigrant family. Give them something special and heartwarming to get excited about. OtterBox, in northern Colorado, has an annual competition called Otter Cares, where different employee groups raise money and host events for different nonprofit organizations. It is about the money but also the impact on the OtterBox organization. OtterBox's employees get pretty pumped and it creates substantial impact on the company's culture and employee pride.

This mission-focused attitude should also be in alignment with your *why* and creates loyal, inspired, and "unrecruitable" employees—employees who don't want to leave.

Five: Show your Appreciation

Give your employees your time, thanks, and appreciation. A pat on the back now and then is a great way to create value. Every employee wants a boss who appreciates their employees and shows it.

If you can create an environment where your employees feel supported, challenged, trusted, and are given all the tools they need to succeed, then you will have an abundance of qualified and valu-

Value-Aligned Leadership

able applicants—and no more worries that finding good employees is difficult.

Competency #5: Focus on Creating Value, Constantly

Remember your first love? Remember you couldn't stop thinking about them and being with them? Your mind was constantly looking for ways to grow that love, to sustain that love and those feelings. In a very practical way, you were always thinking and looking for ways to grow that value—love.

This is a personal, nonbusiness example, but it is a good illustration of the passion you feel when getting totally involved and committed to something outside of yourself. When you are always thinking, and looking for ways to grow value, you can do exactly that.

Walk around the office or facility and just look. Open your mind and imagination. Look at a process or people doing a project. Are there ways to improve what they are doing? Can this create additional synergies? Are your meetings producing clarity and success? How can they be more intentional? Does your marketing message clearly communicate your products and services to your customers? Does it communicate clearly the value you bring them? Are your employees happy, do they feel appreciated? Is your building clean and comfortable, and conducive to productivity? Are your employees working hard or are they a little too comfortable?

What you are doing is looking for ways to improve the lives of your employees, customers, and vendors. You are looking for ways where you, and they, can find all sorts of small and large opportunities to build value. Once you open your mind, imagination, and

The Value Equation

heart, you will start seeing significant and lasting value waiting to be created.

Competency #6: Know the Truth

One of the more difficult tasks of leadership is the ability to face the truth—the cold, hard reality—the brutal, honest facts. As an entrepreneur, you may be habitually upbeat and optimistic, which can carry you through very difficult times. Yet sometimes this optimism can become blindness, carelessness, and just plain stubbornness. It is your job and a critical part of your responsibility to know and understand your business's strengths, weaknesses, opportunities, and threats. It is also critical that you know *yourself*.

We all have blind spots. We all tend to play down our weaknesses and inflate our strengths. Yet, in business, the clarity of our knowing exactly where we are, and where we are not, is the first step to creating success. We all need to develop *emotional intelligence*, the ability to understand yourself, recognize the impact of your actions on others, and know the truth. Here are just a few questions to ask yourself and your team.

One: What does your *wake* look like? After a meeting, after a sales call, working with a team on a project, you leave a wake of feelings and a reaction in people. Did you motivate and inspire them, or did you leave them a bit angry and upset? Did you show care and support, or did they feel let down? Did you accomplish what you wanted, yet at the price of frustration and confusion? Do you micromanage out of fear, or do people feel supported and trusted? Give some thought to your wake. It has a much bigger impact on your business and the development of value than you think.

Value-Aligned Leadership

Two: What is it like on the other side of *me*? Is your perception of your personality and your impact accurate? Often your perception of your strengths or weaknesses is not necessarily accurate. We have had clients that perceived of themselves as caring and thoughtful leaders, yet the truth was the opposite. We have had clients that thought they were well liked and admired but were deceiving themselves. Your effectiveness as a leader, as a manager, is proportional to how honestly you know yourself. Get to know what your employees and customers truthfully think of you.

Ask your team members or advisors and be truthful with yourself and open with them. This is tough and sometimes the truth hurts, but remember, you are trying to create value—not egos.

Are your products and services as strong and attractive as you think? Do you rationalize away missed sales or quality problems? Are you really a "market leader"? It can be easy to get caught up in the hyperbole of marketing "speak." But to create strong values, you need to know exactly how good your products and services are. You need to know the truth—so be ready to take full advantage of the assessments in the second step of the Value Equation. This process can reveal what you need to know. Huge value is found in that process.

Do you have unproductive or disruptive employees? Being a leader is hard, and there is no harder task than letting an employee go. Yet it must be done. For the company's sake, their sake, and your other employees' sakes. Too often this difficult task is put off, but nothing good comes of this and you may find that you have created other, greater problems. Be positive and look for supportive and caring ways to ease the transition. Look for ways to create value in the process—learn from the problem and create new opportunities for other staff.

The Value Equation

Competency #7: Seek Rest

What? Rest?

Life comes at us pretty quick these days, and it is only speeding up! It is tough to schedule downtime.

Yet rest is the catalyst of innovation and value creation. It is during periods of rest that your sense of satisfaction, joy, and fulfillment are the most enjoyable—and sometimes only then do you realize them. For many successful business owners and executives, it is during a hike in the woods or sitting on the beach that inspirations and creative ideas come to mind. It is only when you stop and shut down a bit that you can think or meditate or grow.

No matter how busy you are, you must find the time to stop and relax. It is almost impossible to be creative when you are constantly running and in firefighting mode. Yet that is where many business owners usually are.

Rest is critical to our businesses and our lives. Many years ago, I was struck with an extremely transformative concept of rest—one that changed completely how I now do business. Stay tuned, I'll have more on this in the Epilogue.

Summary

The concepts covered here are not an exhaustive list, nor are they the last word on leadership. Yet I know, beyond any doubt, that these seven will have a huge effect on how you lead and will bring significant value and fulfillment to your life.

If you stop and think about these concepts, you will note that none of them really are about you as the leader, or about helping you find value, significance, and fulfillment. No, the focus of this chapter is about helping your employees—an important group of your stakeholders—find ways to create value and success. Yet helping and serving them will create *significantly* more value and satisfaction then you will ever create on your own. If you as leader serve them, they will create value for your business—which will create significant value for you.

Notes

1. Lencioni, Patrick. *The Advantage: Why Organizational Health Trumps Everything Else in Business.* Jossey-Bass, 2012.
2. Ibid., p. 15.

7

VALUE EQUATION STORIES OF SUCCESS

> "But when a company clearly communicates their WHY, what they believe, and we believe what they believe, then we will sometimes go to extraordinary lengths to include those products or brands in our lives. This is not because they are better, but because they become markers or symbols of the values and beliefs we hold dear."
>
> —Simon Sinek, *Start with Why*

So, what really happens when the leaders of a company experience the Value Equation process, and what are the ultimate changes that occur? What benefits, what transformations can it actually produce for your business?

Simply put: If you applied these principles to your business because you don't have the fulfillment, the enjoyment, or the success you want, your business will look completely different—what you do every day will be different, many of your customers will be different, your finances will look different. Your business's focus would

The Value Equation

not be about making money or profit. You would see your way to align your core values, transform your business, and create *sustainable* success that brings you great satisfaction and joy.

The money would be a byproduct, but it will be there too. In order to achieve financial success, you can't look at the money—you have to look at the meaning behind what you do, and the importance of it to your customers.

True transformation! One dictionary definition of *transformation* as a "change in form, appearance, nature, or character."[1] That is our hope—that is exactly what Steve and I would love to see—that your business would change in form, appearance, nature, and character. That your employees would embrace your vision and values and become truly *unrecruitable*—because there's nowhere else they would rather be. Your customers would love what you do and buy from you to the point that you have no *real* competition. And you, as the business owner or leader, would feel fulfilled and joyful. *That* would be transformation.

In this book, we have defined the *why,* the *what,* and the *how*—the basics of the process that we call the Value Equation. In summary then, how does transformation actually happen? What results have been achieved by businesses that implement the Value Equation?

Value Equation Stories of Success

Transformation occurs when these things happen:

1. You are ready and willing to invest the time to work on your business and not just *in* it. It all starts with you.
2. You understand and can articulate your core values.
3. You know where you are headed. Transformation can only happen when your picture of success is clear, articulated, measurable, and communicated appropriately.
4. You understand, can articulate, and can achieve your Key Growth Factors in full alignment with your management team and employees.
5. Your business goals, practices, and outcomes are in alignment with your core values.
6. Your employees, customers, vendors, and other stakeholders understand and embrace your values and your *why*.
7. You become a true servant leader to your employees and other stakeholders and not just a boss.

Your transformational results should look like these:

1. The character, substance, and financial performance of your business will be completely different from your current state.
2. Your fear dissipates and is replaced with confidence, joy, and fulfillment—and the passion is back.
3. The organizational health of your company—the morale, cohesion, and communication of your employees—is solid and exciting.
4. You have more time.
5. Your business is growing dramatically.
6. The financial performance of your business has improved. You have more cash, little or no debt, and have working capital to support your growth.
7. You are living out your core values and making a true impact on the world around you.

The Value Equation

These results are not some fantasy or pipe dream. You *can* achieve some really fun and exciting results and create a community, instead of just a place to work. The first step is to get started.

The Value Equation has been around for almost 20 years. Those of us at Agora are pretty excited about the way we have been able to assist in this transformational process and build value for many companies. Here are some examples of actual client companies that have been truly transformed, with significant results achieved. The names of the individuals in these stories have been altered to protect their personal and company confidentiality.

The Transformation of a General Contractor

During our consulting tenure with this company, the hands-on leadership changed, the identified customers and marketing strategy was altered completely, and the company culture underwent a radical shift to be more open and with more multidirectional communication than it ever had before. People's lives were changed, they experienced more joy and significance, the company's net income more than tripled, and the employees are now excited about the company they work for and embrace its future vision and values.

This client, Bill, was a general contractor who built higher-end homes in a few subdivisions of a growing area of California. Bill owned the company with two others—Pete and Andrew. I met with Bill and as we "talked business" like most of us do, he expressed all sorts of problems and issues that were causing Bill's frustration. He was stressed, overworked, and felt the pressure of "keeping the business together." The more we talked, the more I realized Bill's company was slowing dying.

Value Equation Stories of Success

As is our standard practice, we spent a lot of time initially observing the business operations and asking questions to try and understand the real issues. Here are some of the key takeaways:

- Their revenue had been flat for five years and their gross profit and net income had been slowly falling during that time.
- The three owners of the business had differing thoughts on where the business should head, and they each had different personal goals.
- They could not really define what the goals of their business were. With no long-term vision, they were pretty much in day-to-day survival mode (i.e., building enough homes to pay the bills).
- The company literally had no vision, *why*, or purpose that anyone—employees, vendors, or customers—could embrace.
- Business development efforts were stagnant—they were chasing revenue by answering RFQs.
- There was little clarity on who, exactly, their customers were or what their customer's real needs and desires were.
- The intercompany communication was poor.
- They had a good team of employees with good skills, but their employees were confused as to the company's goals or objectives.
- The productivity and quality of the company workforce wasn't bad, but their turnover was high. With no real reason to stay, carpenters and others left when a slightly better opportunity presented itself.
- Company morale wasn't bad, and they were good, skilled folks, but confused and frustrated.

The Value Equation

The frustration of the owners and employees, the flat revenue and falling profit, the lack of excitement and joy, and the employee turnover were simply the symptoms of a larger problem. With no clarity on a greater purpose and goal, there was no intentional effort to build any significant value.

Painting a Picture of Success

The first priority was to help the business develop a picture of success. What would the owners like to create? What was their greater purpose and why? What values, specifically, would they like to live and work by, in their business?

We started by helping them define their core values. First the three owners, and then the management team. It was no surprise to us, but very surprising to them, to see that most of their core values were shared by the three owners and those of the management team as well. You should have seen the looks on their faces when they saw how much alignment there was! They all wanted more clarity, trust, and teamwork. Everyone wanted the company's reputation to be based on exceptional quality, but also creativity and innovation. These were the values that needed to be intentionally driven through the company to their customers, the values that needed to be created for the owners and managers to feel successful.

One value that was not on anyone's top-five list was profit. This was interesting. It just wasn't a big priority. Growth was . . . but not profit. Everyone seemed to have this intuition that if they focused on delivering quality, creativity, and innovation, the money would come.

Next, we needed to work with the owners to define success, in alignment to their core values. What were their long-term goals?

Value Equation Stories of Success

What did they want to achieve? Here is where some difficulty developed, as Andrew had a different view on a definition of success. The process took several months of work to create a picture of success, and eventually Andrew decided to move in a different direction and sold his interest in the company to Bill and Pete.

> **You need alignment to get buy-in, and you need buy-in to create value.**

This move ultimately enabled alignment for the other two owners. Alignment of long-term goals and how success is defined is critical to the success of any company. Owners, especially, and the management need to be in agreement about where the company is headed.

The success factors they originally came up with contained some very aggressive goals. Growth was their number one item—they wanted to double the revenue of the company *in two years*. In addition, they wanted a *why*—their reason for being in business—that could be embraced not only by their employees but by their customers as well. Quality was big, but everyone, every company, wants to be known for quality. They wanted to also be known as a creative and innovative builder. They believed they could excite their customers with their creative and innovative designs, solutions, and use of space. It was fun to see the excitement and creativity as the team developed the plans to begin delivering on these values and grow their business. I wanted them to dream big—and they did!

The *why* success factor that everyone embraced was to have a greater purpose. Something that would add significance and enrich-

The Value Equation

ment to the company and its employees and provide for the greater good of the local community.

But what did a mission-focused purpose look like? How is that created? How does that create value for the company? The employees? They looked in the community for a nonprofit organization that fit their goals. Eventually everyone rallied around an organization providing practical electrical, plumbing, welding, and woodworking education for disadvantaged youth. This was a warmhearted story. I would love to sit and hear their employees tell the stories about how they helped transform lives.

Key Growth Factors

As we worked through the business assessment, many issues surfaced. You can see many of them in the above observations. However, there were two significant problems that really were at the heart of their lack of success. One, the flat revenue and two, the lack of clear communications with employees. Fixing those two issues became their primary Key Growth Factors and the focus for their initial 100 Day Plan—and in turn, these had huge effects on their business.

Bill and Pete really wanted to see the business not just grow, but become successful and deliver on their values. The owners understood that growth was simply the byproduct of success, yet initially they were at a loss as to how to solve the problem. They had been so focused on chasing revenue and keeping everyone busy they had lost sight of the market and what their customers really wanted. Not to mention that their profit margins were horrible when all they had to compete on is price.

Value Equation Stories of Success

The company spent quite a bit of time working through their initial business development plan. The focus of their time was spent on two items. One, a deep customer and market survey and two, a Blue Ocean assessment and plan. These two tools helped them create a plan to deliver significant value to their customers, increase their sales price and gross profit margin, and create significant differentiation.

The company did a great job on their customer surveys and Blue Ocean assessments and planning. They came up with a very creative idea that created significant differentiation from the other builders in the area. In their surveys, they learned that homeowners placed a high value on making their homes as livable as possible in their first year of ownership. Question—how could they assist in this after the sale? In the Blue Ocean process, they came up with an innovative idea: What if they helped the new homeowner over that year with fixes and changes, to make them as happy and comfortable as possible? So, they did.

They called their new warranty/guarantee program the 100% Happiness Guarantee. If the homeowner wanted to change the color of a wall—no problem. If they wanted a cabinet put in the laundry room—they did that. If they wanted a different bathroom faucet—well, they did that as well. All at no additional cost! And they fixed any construction defects, again at no cost, for a full year.

Of course, there was a dollar limit on the changes, but their customers loved it. Their reputation and brand *soared*. They focused on their top values of trust, quality, creativity, and innovation, and they certainly delivered Wow!

Employee communication was also pretty poor at the start of this project. The management team were in the dark about major

The Value Equation

decisions because the ownership team micromanaged everyone because of their fear—their survival values were being threatened. People would show up to meetings with no notebook, reports, or plans. There was little accountability, so they didn't bother. In spite of having good people, the owners thought they needed to make all of the decisions.

It is always difficult to explain to business leaders that perhaps they are not as strong or as liked as they think—and this situation was no different. However, the two remaining owners were motivated to truly transform their business and they made a huge effort to be open, creative, and spend the time to make the significant changes necessary. In the midst of the fires and struggles, it was natural to jump in and do . . . something. Yet Bill and Pete, to their credit, took the time to seek answers and creative solutions to their business problems. They created a separate Success Factor Grid focused solely on the company's organizational health to address the issues.

The two Key Growth Factors on their initial organizational health Success Factor Grid were to ensure that all employees felt like part of a successful and fun company, and to empower all employees so they could create and succeed.

Their focus and actions completely changed their business. Clarity produced trust, which produced action, which produced creativity, which produced innovation, which produced growing success—which produced fun!

Once people began to understand the focus and feel wanted, involved, and empowered, they created a much more enjoyable and energetic work environment. They began to embrace the company's *why* and their future—and the more momentum and success they had, the more excited people felt.

Value Equation Stories of Success

The First 100-Day Plan

The initial 100-Day Plan focused on the new business development plan: clearly understanding their customers' needs and creating some innovative programs to differentiate themselves from the other builders in the area, and addressing the communication problems. They didn't focus on revenue or cash flow, or even operational issues—those would come. If they could become a trusting and empowered team, and clearly understand how to build homes that families would be excited to own, then they could begin to create momentum and that would build and create success.

Success

As the company began to intentionally focus on creating and delivering their core values through the business, those values started to create better communication and employee support. Everyone became focused on creating value rather than watching it dissipate. At first, they took on significant risk and a financial hit to implement the 100% Happiness Guarantee—but the results were stunning and created a true "Blue Ocean" (non-competitive position) for them.

Here are a few of the transformational results they achieved over a four-year period. As the business began to build momentum and the employees began to embrace the changes, Bill's fear disappeared and was replaced with confidence and joy. The organizational health improved to the point that they became *the* contractor to work for! Hey, everyone loves a winner.

Their innovative and creative homes became the rage and produced dramatic growth. The success of the business created signifi-

The Value Equation

cant cash flow and working capital, and net income *tripled*. Bill and Pete have more time—and both were able to take a *couple* of two week vacations each year!

Bill, Pete, and their employees created success by living out their core values. It was difficult at first, and results did not come over night—but their commitment, creativity, and intentional focus eventually created some really cool value.

Teamwork Requires Relationships

Michael was an investment advisor with a nationally known financial advisory firm. He had his own office and a single assistant. He was outgoing, knowledgeable, and understood his business well.

He enjoyed the Value Equation process and gained significant insight into where he could bring discipline and focus to gain additional success. Michael's business was doing fairly well but not great, and he really thought he could do much better. We helped him develop both short-term and longer-term goals. He was fairly clear about some of the goals on his list, but he was also fairly aggressive. During the assessment phase of the process, we found that he was pretty much hitting all of the right items. From a sales, marketing, client development, and operational standpoint, he was doing well. However, we also noticed one odd little thing, which ended up being a major key to his success.

Michael's administrative assistant, Robin, had great people skills and was very engaging. However, Michael didn't see her role as being involved in the actual services he provided to his customers, and he was very focused on achieving his goals. He would greet her each morning and then go in his office and shut the door. When

Value Equation Stories of Success

she tried to connect with him on a personal level, talking about her family and asking questions of him, he felt those interactions were a waste of time and didn't really respond to her. So, she answered phones, took messages, and greeted customers, but she didn't feel that Michael appreciated her capabilities or cared about her. She didn't know what his business goals were and had no visibility into the business. She felt "shut out."

We noticed this lack of interaction, which was surprising given that they were both outgoing, friendly people. We brought this to Michael's attention and asked him to try spending a little time getting to know Robin and build more of a relationship with her—let her know he appreciated that she was there and cared about her. So he did, and as they interacted more, it became natural for him to talk about where he was going with the business and what was happening with the individual clients. Those interactions energized Robin, and she felt empowered because he was sharing this information with her. She also felt a sense of psychological safety in her job that had been lacking. Michael began to listen and respond to Robin's suggestions for improved client support and business development. They *communicated* and built a relationship, both on a professional and business level.

As a result, Robin became more aligned with Michael's goals and could support him in providing services to their customers—and they became a team. They started working together to achieve his goals, which became *their* goals.

We finished the project and watched as Michael's business accelerated as a result of the changed environment in the office. The

The Value Equation

Michael-and-Robin team was doing well, creating value for his clients and for themselves as well.

I had lunch with Michael one day in June, halfway through the year, to connect with him and find out how he was doing with his goals.

"I'm done," he said.

I asked, "What do you mean, you're done?"

"I've met all my goals for the year already."

As you can imagine, I was stunned—it was surprising that addressing the one odd little thing we noticed about his business was so effective in meeting his goals. His personal connection with Robin empowered not only her but their teamwork, and they became aligned in providing outstanding service to their customers. That communication was one of the keys—a Key Growth Factor—to meeting his business goals and Success Factors. His customers felt that they had not only Michael helping them, but a *team*—and as an aligned team, they were much more effective in meeting and exceeding customer expectations.

Michael's practice is now being used by the investment firm as an example success story for their other advisors, and he shares what he did to achieve his growth with others—which was communicate his values and his goals with his team and align his team to achieve the Success Factors he had identified. Sometimes it is the seemingly inconsequential things that bring success!

When in Rome—Hire Romans

A California company that built semiconductor manufacturing equipment had designed a conveyor system to move front opening

Value Equation Stories of Success

unified pods (FOUPs), which were the containers 300 mm silicon wafers were stored in for transport in the production line. They had a phenomenal AMHS (automated machine handling system) conveyor, but they hadn't sold a single system. As I worked through the Value Equation process with them and got to know their product and their market, I recognized a misalignment with their company location and that of their customers.

The AMHS was very complicated and required considerable customer interaction to function. Sixty percent of their customers were in Taiwan, and yet the engineering design and test systems were in California. This required that a potential customer had to send a large group of its precious engineering resources to California for a significant time to check out and work with the material handling system—a major sales hurdle. In addition, the engineers in California who designed and engineered the system didn't speak Mandarin Chinese.

The company had briefly looked at the idea of creating some sort of engineering and sales team in Taiwan, but due to a variety of complex issues, that idea never got off the ground. One day in a brainstorming session I asked, "Why don't we find a Taiwanese company that can help us not only engineer, but also demonstrate and show the conveyor system, in proximity to all the semiconductor factories?" Everyone sort of chuckled at me . . . but no one laughed!

The manager of the AMHS group and I met and began to look at the idea and its complexities. The first thing we did was put together a set of Success Factor Grids. This was of primary importance. We needed to understand in depth what was needed to create success with our potential project. Missing a critical item

The Value Equation

on one of our grids could spell disaster, not to mention the money and time involved. The primary Key Growth Factor was to find a Taiwanese partner company that could fill a majority of their identified Success Factors.

Three Success Factors were critical. One, they needed a strong team of semiconductor processing, AMHS, and software experts; two, they also wanted a group that knew the management of the fabrication plants. They not only wanted to create a cool and innovate FOUP transportation system—but they also wanted to sell them as well. Lastly, they needed to find a Taiwanese partner that shared the same values. In particular, the intellectual property laws in Taiwan at the time were not as stringent and as enforceable as in the U.S. To be blunt, they needed a partner they could trust. This required an intensive study to align the partner's needs and their needs, to be able to sell the system, support it, and protect it, exceptionally well.

To make a long story short, after several months of searching, we did help them find a Taiwanese gentleman who shared their values and owned a company of engineering talent that fit their needs. They looked at several firms with excellent possibilities, but having a clear and complete Success Factor Grid helped them find the right fit—and he and his company turned out to be an amazing fit.

When they moved the conveyor system into Taiwan and had it working and operating, the engineering people from customer companies could go play with the conveyor system and really see its potential, without investing resources in travel to California. The Value Equation process helped them understand the elements nec-

Value Equation Stories of Success

essary for success and lowered their risk potential significantly—especially identifying the importance of having shared values around intellectual property. The process aligned everyone from the AMHS group, the company executives, and their new Taiwanese partner. The resulting clarity was a huge part of their success.

The first year the company introduced the conveyer system in California, there were no sales. That first year in Taiwan, they had revenue of $20 million, and the next year they sold almost $50 million of conveyor systems. It was explosive.

Summary

The business leaders in these stories shared two very important characteristics—they were unhappy with the state of their businesses and were willing to invest the time and discipline needed to create change, value, and deeper fulfillment. That is the most important ingredient required to create sustainable value with the Value Equation process. Much of what we request of people in the process is not complicated, but it does require time and discipline.

Transformation happens not because you want change, but because you are *willing* to change.

Regrettably, most business men and women who are struggling don't believe they need help. Some are willing to change but just "can't find the time" to take that first step. Unfortunately, statistics show that the number of businesses that fail are startling. According to the Bureau of Labor Statistics, approximately 500,000 new businesses are started each year, and about 500,000 others close down each year. Most new businesses fail within 3-5 years.[2]

The Value Equation

The reasons for failure are as varied as the businesses themselves. But the patterns of success show a surprising familiar trend . . . leadership engagement with clear, concise, and aligned values throughout the business processes . . . from manufacturing to retail sales. The key is to act, to engage, to be willing to transform.

Notes

1. *Dictionary.com,* s.v. "transformation," accessed November 21, 2017. http://www.dictionary.com/browse/transformation?s=t
2. Bureau of Labor Statistics, Business Employment Dynamics.

EPILOGUE

REST—VALUE RESTORED

> That person is like a tree planted by streams of water, which yields its fruit in season and whose leaf does not wither—whatever they do prospers.
>
> —Psalm 1:3 NIV

Several years ago, I was sitting on the balcony of our hotel room, overlooking an absolutely beautiful early summer morning in Monterey, California. The gray of the morning fog was just beginning to dissipate into the greens and browns of the manicured golf course laid out before me. The wind quietly and gently blew past my chair and I was glad for the fleece I had on. The boys were still asleep, and Mary was tucked in with a cup of coffee and a book, so I had the time completely to myself. Quiet, peaceful, a time of rest—a rarity I think you can appreciate.

We had flown from Colorado a few days before for our annual family vacation. Just Mary and I and our two sons. A week of golf,

The Value Equation

hikes in the hills, walks on the beach, and family fun. Well, at least that was the idea. Developing and executing acquisition and merger strategies for client companies, I never really had much time for a quiet vacation. The search for the right company and closing the deal were constantly filling my thoughts and broke down any separation between my work life and family life.

Anyway, there was never much time to just *rest*, and this vacation was no exception. I made it out with everyone to California, but several calls every day interrupted our time together. But that's the nature of the job, and on this particular week, I was coming close to completing a large acquisition.

But somehow this morning was different, and I was able to find the time for a little peace and quiet. My hometown of Pacific Grove was just down the road and I began to quietly reminisce and soak in the sweet memories, sights, and sounds. It was quiet, except for the songs of birds and some greenkeepers off in the distance.

As I sat there, a voice entered my mind, almost as if someone had just spoken. "Stop . . . " I was so sure someone had spoken that I looked around me. Nothing. Then a little louder: "Be quiet, listen." Again, nothing there—just me and the morning fog. The thought that I was hearing things didn't spoil my quiet time—for some reason, the voice was incredibly peaceful.

But the message changed everything. I knew, right then and there, exactly what it meant. It was something I needed to hear. It spoke right to the depths of my heart.

As time went by over the next several months, that message would come back to me and make me intentionally pause. Many times each week, especially lying in bed at night, I would ponder,

Rest—Value Restored

not just what it meant, but what I needed to heed, what I needed to do. It was a call to action, a call to life.

We all live in such a busy world, constantly bombarded by noise and information. News, traffic, markets, news talk, financial advice, family advice, the next toy, the next vacation, new technology, new ways to live and thrive, new diets, cooking and exercise fads. Sports, movies, Facebook, CNN, the latest HBO epic. The *constant noise of life* . . . or perhaps more accurately, a *constant life of noise*.

The pressure to work hard, to keep going at an incredibly tense, frantic pace is constant. More and more is demanded. The competition might gain sales on us, customers might switch to competitors, perhaps our price points are too high. So, we fight hard, push hard, and even manipulate a bit.

We work hard for "success," increasing revenues, more market share, higher profit. Yet, we never quite question whether these measures of business success and the corresponding pace of life is sustainable. It is a never-ending cycle on the crazy merry-go-round of business . . . and the stress is killing us and clouding our true goals.

So we check out, we escape. TV, romance novels, toys, free time, recreational activities, and the outdoors. We fill our time off with cool stuff and we are busy . . . really busy, and the pace of life is not slowing down. It is almost a cultural disease.

I acknowledge that life is not all bad. We do make a living, it's fun to watch the kids enjoy sports, grow up, and achieve success. We like our toys and vacations. Okay, life is full.

Ask anyone how they are doing and they answer, "I'm really busy." But pay attention to what they don't say . . . "I'm excited

The Value Equation

because the business is growing; we've reached milestones of successful innovation and our customers love it; our employees are our best recruiters." Or, alternatively, "My life is full of (insert what you'd like your life to be full of . . . joy, adventure, family, growth, wisdom, peace)."

Are you creating long-term, sustainable *value in your business and your life?* Joy, peace, innovation, credibility, integrity, love. Can you identify those things in your life that you really create? Is your life and work producing a sense of value, of fulfillment—or is it just stuff?

It doesn't seem like it now, but there will always be the next deal, contract, new product, new car, TV series, or baseball game. There is nothing wrong with your stuff, but the danger is that you just get carried along in the current of life and never stop to consider where this is taking you . . . or more importantly, how this stuff is adding to your personal *values*. Will this new car make you see more truth or humility . . . will this new product add integrity to your product line?

So . . .

Stop.

Be quiet.

Listen.

Stop and take some time to consider what is important to you . . . really important. Stop and be quiet. Let the noise of this world fade away—get away from the intrusion of the noise. Be quiet so you can hear yourself think. And then listen. Listen to your heart. Listen to the deeper things going on inside your head. Listen to that

Rest—Value Restored

quiet little voice that has been nudging you but has been drowned out by all of the noise.

You need to stop all of the crazy and relentless doing and just *be*. Be you, be alone, be quiet. Stop and think, meditate, pray, daydream . . . focus on who you are. And who you want to be.

It is only when you stop, be quiet, and listen that relaxation, recovery, and refreshment come—that true insight happens. It's in this quiet that you are able to actually think . . . clearly, honestly, and from the heart. That is where true and significant and sustainable value comes from. From the heart. Not society's headlong rush, not the life-filling stuff or the escape from life, but from the heart.

The goal of the Value Equation is to encourage you to be intentional, creative, and thoughtful in aligning your *values* with your actions, business or personal, in creating success that increases the value of your business and life. Your true and core values will be fulfilling and sustainable. Those that excite your heart and soul. The result will be that you will know where you are headed, where you want to go, what you want to do, and what you want to be.

The first step is to stop, be quiet, and listen. This is the essence of rest, a forgotten value in today's life. Rest. Take that first step to unplug and rest—to be quiet and just sit and listen. To go for a walk, unplug, and rest. If you want to create value, sustainable value, you need rest.

Find a way to arrange your days so that you are experiencing a joy and contentment in your everyday life. Not just on vacation or at play, but every day. To rest and allow your heart and that small quiet voice to speak to you.

The Value Equation

My personal and professional transformation has been huge—and it has been challenging as well. One, Agora has gone from a one-man operation to a group of amazing and competent colleagues. Having additional staff has changed my focus to their development and success while retaining my own consulting clients, yet a larger team gives us additional resources and capabilities that I never had as a sole practitioner—and the value of our business has increased!

Two, as I have intentionally taken the time to create the value of rest in my life I have become less stressed, more relaxed, less worried, and much happier. I used to work really hard, trying to make things work. Now I work smarter, more intentional, and with greater creativity. Making money used to be a major focus of my stress and worry—I let go of that one. Now I simply focus on building value for our clients. The more value we build, the more income we earn. Simple—and it's a lot more enjoyable.

I enjoy the little things more—the times in the mountains, walks with my wife, and a beer with friends. The time of reflection and rest has been sweet for my family, but it has also helped Agora develop better tools and be more creative in creating value for our clients and workshop participants.

Less stress, better health, more innovative tools, more value for our clients, increased value in our company, more enjoyment . . . not bad for a fairly simple concept!

Rest, the ultimate tool for creating significant and sustaining value—in your work, your life, and your heart.

RECOMMENDED READING

While there are many excellent books on business planning, strategy and leadership, here are some of the best. Some of these were referenced within chapters, but I list them all here for easy access.

Chouinard, Yvon. *Let my People Go Surfing.* Penguin Books, 2016.

Cloud, Henry. *Integrity.* HarperCollins, 2006.

Collins, Jim. *Good to Great.* Harper Collins, 2001.

Fagerlin, Richard. *Trustology.* Wise Guys Press, 2013.

Greenleaf, Robert. *Servant Leadership.* Paulist Press, 2002.

Hutchinson, Chris. *Ripple, A Field Manual for Leadership That Works.* Lasting Impact Press, 2015.

Kim, W. Chan and Renée Mauborgne. *Blue Ocean Strategy: How to Create Uncontested Market Space and Make the Competition Irrelevant.* Harvard Business Review Press, Expanded Edition, 2015.

The Value Equation

Kouzes, James and Barry Posner. *The Leadership Challenge: How to Make Extraordinary Things Happen in Organizations.* Jossey-Bass, 6th edition, April 2017.

Lencioni, Patrick. *The Advantage: Why Organizational Health Trumps Everything Else in Business.* Jossey-Bass, 2012.

Lencioni, Patrick. *The Four Obsessions of an Extraordinary Executive: A Leadership Fable.* Jossey-Bass, 2000.

Sinek, Simon. *Start with Why: How Great Leaders Inspire Everyone to Take Action.* Portfolio: Reprint edition, 2011.

APPENDIX

THE VALUE EQUATION ROAD MAP

The Value Equation Process

Identify Core Values + Paint a Picture of Success + Assess Current Position + Create a Plan = SUCCESS

Personal and Business Values Hierarchy

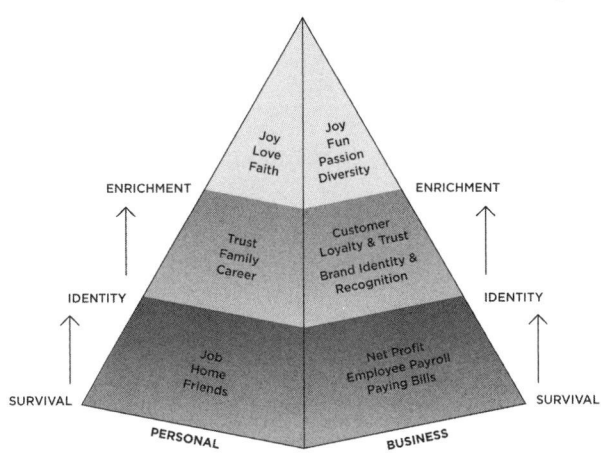

ENRICHMENT
- Joy, Love, Faith
- Joy, Fun, Passion, Diversity

IDENTITY
- Trust, Family, Career
- Customer Loyalty & Trust, Brand Identity & Recognition

SURVIVAL
- Job, Home, Friends
- Net Profit, Employee Payroll, Paying Bills

PERSONAL | BUSINESS

The Value Equation

Characteristics of Fear-Driven Companies

Fear-Driven	Plan- and Values-Driven
Confusion, reactive management	Clarity, purpose, proactive management
Lack of trust	Trust, teamwork
Controlling management, micromanagement	Freedom, independence, responsibility
Worry, stress	Confidence
Present focus, problem focus	Future focus, strategic focus
Low employee morale	High employee morale
High employee turnover	High employee loyalty and retention (making them nonrecruitable)
Poor or declining financial performance	Good financial results

Characteristics of Northern Colorado Businesses

OtterBox	Walker Manufacturing	Fort Collins Wind Symphony
Golden rule Treat others the way you want to be treated.	Respect for employees and their families.	Making a substantial contribution to the musical life of members and patrons.
Passion A burning desire to win.	Keep promises and pursue excellence.	Giving audiences memorable performance experiences.
Innovation Have the courage to find new ways to solve life's problems.	Lead by serving.	Assist in the music education of young people.
Integrity Do the right thing, the right way, even when no one is watching.	Always love people.	Provide members with an opportunity for musical expression, growth, and fellowship.
Giving back To whom much is given, much is expected. We grow to give.	Manufacturing with integrity.	And fun, don't forget the fun!

Appendix

Value Equation Step 1: Identify Your Core Values

The Value Equation Process

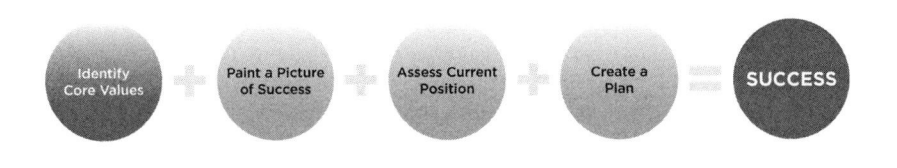

Identify Core Values + Paint a Picture of Success + Assess Current Position + Create a Plan = SUCCESS

Some Examples of Core Values

Core Values			
Clarity	Love	Security	Joy
Sincerity	Forgiveness	Humility	Truth
Creativity	Diversity	Wisdom	Credibility
Kindness	Passion	Respect	Creativity

Value Equation Tool @www.AgoraConsulting.us

Core Values Exercise – Two thoughtful exercises you can do to help you determine your most important values.

The Value Equation

Value Equation Step 2: Painting a Picture of Success

The Value Equation Process

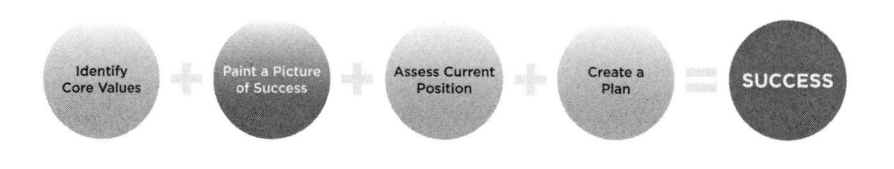

Identify Core Values + Paint a Picture of Success + Assess Current Position + Create a Plan = SUCCESS

A Simple Picture of Success

Personal	Business	Financial	Legacy	Fun
Living a life of no regrets	Sales at $10M 15% net income	No debts	Reputation for integrity	Travel to all 50 states
Still in love . . .	40 loyal and happy employees	Own home	Community giving and involvement	Jump out of an airplane
Successfully launch the kids	Known as the place to buy . . .	Reasonable retirement resources	Providing meaningful jobs	Have one really crazy adventure!

Example Success Factor Grid: Long-Term Business Values Created

Financial	Products	Leadership	Organizational Health	Reputation
Abundance	Growth	Vision	Accessibility	Quality
Stability	Innovation	Boldness	Communication	Trust
Financial independence	Integrity	Stewardship	Clarity	Truth
Growing profit	Dependability	Effectiveness	Transparency	Fun

Appendix

Values to Achieve, Avoid, and Preserve

	Achieve	Avoid	Preserve
For my community	Products & services that serve the local community	The fear of saying yes	Opportunities for others
For my employees and coworkers	A work environment people love to be a part of	My strengths being overdone	Relationships that allow us to fail and pivot
For my family	Lasting memories	Kids testing my values and finding them false	Our sense of roots and stability
For my role	Work that uses my full potential	Perception that I don't deliver what I promise	Ownership of my schedule
For . . .	Business value that leads to referrals		

Value Equation Tools @ www.AgoraConsulting.us

Painting a Picture of Success/Success Factor Grids – Examples of ways to "Paint a Picture" or define and articulate success with our Success Factor Grid tools.

    a. **SFG** – Long-Term Objectives and Goals

    b. **SFG** – Business Development (Sales) Objectives and Goals

    c. **SFG** – Long-Term Values Integration

    d. **SFG** – Items, Goals, Values to Achieve, Avoid, and Preserve

Value Equation Step 3: Assessing Your Current Practices and Outcomes

The Value Equation Process

Identify Core Values + Paint a Picture of Success + Assess Current Position + Create a Plan = SUCCESS

Value Equation Tools @www.AgoraConsulting.us

Values Assessment Scorecard – A scorecard for assessing how well you are doing in creating and executing your core values in your business.

Business Assessment Scorecard – A scorecard for assessing the capability, health, strengths, and weaknesses of your business.

Appendix

Example Values Assessment Scorecard

Top Values	Personal Score	Leadership Team Score	Key Employee Score	Key Advisor Score	Customer or Client Score
Financial					
Abundance	2.5	3	3	2.5	
Stability	2	3	3	2.5	
Financial Independence	1.5	1.5	1.5	1	
Growing profit	1.5	2	2	2	
Products					
Growth					2.5
Innovation					3
Integrity					3.5
Dependability					3
Leadership					
Vision					
Boldness					
Stewardship					
Effectiveness					
Organizational Health					
Accessibility					
Communication					
Clarity					
Transparency					
Reputation					
Quality					
Trust					
Truth					
Fun					

The Value Equation

Business Assessment Scorecard

Assessment Areas	Personal Score	Leadership Team Score	Key Employee Score	Customer or Client Score
Business Position				
Market				
Products and Services				
Credibility				
Revenue/Business Development				
Competition				
Customer Satisfaction				
Customer Satisfaction				
Product Delivery				
Product Quality				
Leadership and Management				
Vision				
Leadership				
Communication of Vision				
Clarity of Internal Communication				
Strength of Management Team				
Accountability				
Overall Employee Health				
Business Planning				
Business Planning				
Financial Planning				
Product Development, Production & Quality				
Shop Planning and Organization				
Shop Management				
Shop Quality and Delivery				
Tools, Equipment, Facilities				
Financial Position				
Financial Strength				
Gross Profit Margin				
Net Income				
Cash and Working Capital				
Assets				
Liabilities and Debt				
Future Growth and Direction				
Growth Potential				
Capital Required				
Return on Investment Potential				

Appendix

Value Equation Step 4: Defining Your Key Growth Factors to Develop Your Plan

The Value Equation Process

Identify Core Values + Paint a Picture of Success + Assess Current Position + Create a Plan = SUCCESS

Example 100-Day Plan

Key Growth Factors and Priority	100-Day Action Plan	Long-Term Success Factors	Core Values
1. Improve Sales		$10M in Revenue	Abundance Growth

The Value Equation

100-Day Plan: Action Column Complete

Key Growth Factors and Priority	100-Day Action Plan	Long-Term Success Factors	Core Values
1. Improve sales	• Blue Ocean strategy • Customer interviews • Team brainstorming	$10M in revenue	Abundance Growth
2. Improve organization and communication	• Publish vision statement • Implement management team monthly assessment and communication meeting	40 loyal and happy employees	Communication Vision Clarity Truth
3. Equip all employees with all the tools they need to succeed	• Conduct employee and management interviews to assess needs	40 loyal and happy employees	Accessibility Trust Boldness Stewardship Effectiveness
4. Focus on creating additional gross profit margin to increase cash	• Perform detailed operations assessment to find Key Growth Factors • Create plan (SFG) for operations	$10M in revenue with 15% net profit	Stability Growing profit Financial freedom
5. Improve product quality and delivery	• Hire QA manager • Implement QA plan	Known as *"the* place to buy"	Quality Innovation Integrity Dependability

Value Equation Tools @www.AgoraConsulting.us

100-Day Plan – A focused and intentional short-term plan to assist you in implementing your initial Success Factors and aligning business practices to your core values.

Appendix

Value Equation Step 5: Review, Assess, Adjust, and Keep Going

The Value Equation Process

Identify Core Values + Paint a Picture of Success + Assess Current Position + Create a Plan = SUCCESS

Value-Aligned Leadership Competencies

1. It's not about you
2. Start with *why*
3. Communicate with clarity
4. Develop great people
5. Focus on creating value, constantly
6. Know the truth
7. Seek rest

The Value Equation

Transformation occurs when these things happen:

1. You are ready and willing to invest the time to work on your business and not just *in* it. It all starts with you.
2. You understand and can articulate your core values.
3. You know where you are headed. Transformation can only happen when your picture of success is clear, articulated, measurable, and communicated appropriately.
4. You understand, can articulate, and can achieve your Key Growth Factors in full alignment with your management team and employees.
5. Your business goals, practices, and outcomes are in alignment with your core values.
6. Your employees, customers, vendors, and other stakeholders understand and embrace your values and your *why*.
7. You become a true servant leader to your employees and other stakeholders and not just a boss.

Your transformational results should look like these:

1. The character, substance, and financial performance of your business will be completely different from your current state.
2. Your fear dissipates and is replaced with confidence, joy, and fulfillment—and the passion is back.
3. The organizational health of your company—the morale, cohesion, and communication of your employees—is solid and exciting.
4. You have more time.
5. Your business is growing dramatically.
6. The financial performance of your business has improved. You have more cash, little or no debt, and have working capital to support your growth.
7. You are living out your core values and making a true impact on the world around you.

ACKNOWLEDGMENTS

Steve and I are both thankful and excited to wake up each morning and start a new day. We thank God that we have air in our lungs, health, and the energy to take on life and our work—the Grand Adventure.

From Garry Krum

It has been a significant effort to write this book. It has often been said that it takes a team and many others whose influence, time, and support over the years are critical to any thoughts and ideas being placed on paper—and that is very much the case with this book.

I love what I do. I get tremendous joy from supporting and challenging clients and watching the lightbulbs go on and their businesses bring them fulfillment and success. Most of the concepts and tools in this book have come from several years of working with some amazing business leaders and their companies. There

The Value Equation

have been many successes and a few failures, but it has been a fun ride. To a few that represent many—Scott Groff and Pete Bohley, Carl Lee, Kurt Hoeven, Geoff Ribar, Shane Hunsinger, Maureen Lamb, David Kay, Sam Harrell, Edward Yang, Dr. Gary Ewen and the folks at Colorado Christian University, Michael Stevens, and Michelle Story.

To the members of our various Transform Groups, much thanks and appreciation. Many of the thoughts here were first formally articulated there. I hate to leave any out, but that first group several years ago got things going—Bob Seale, Ron Ahlschwede, Dirk Dykson, Kenny Kramer, but especially to Jonathan Ahlschwede. One gets sweet inspiration, sitting on the side of a 14,000-foot peak. Thanks, Jonathan, for the climbing and dreaming companionship.

Thanks to Agora's Strategic Advisors and Advisory Board. It takes a team to build a business and fulfill a vision—and Josh Schuler has been my right-hand, encourager, and chief challenger since we met at the Jim Collins lecture. Thanks Josh for the thought-provoking talks, good beer, and sharing your time, knowledge, and skills with me—but we aren't done yet!

Special thanks to the team at Aloha Publishing. They have been amazing! Steve and I have been so impressed with their professionalism, thoughtfulness, and personal support. Thank you, Maryanna Young, for the initial spark. You have encouraged and pushed and loved us. Your level of insight and patience with a couple of finance guys has been nothing short of amazing! The success of this effort belongs in large part to you. Thanks also to the editorial team, especially Jennifer Regner. You took a bunch of crazy business concepts

Acknowledgments

and helped us articulate and actually get them into a book. Your patience with me has been awesome.

The marketing team at Aloha has also made this a reality. Their patience in trying to understand, translate, and articulate our complicated business and concepts so others could understand them has been marvelous. Thank you, Melissa Lambert and Marina Alcoser.

I am blessed with a family of readers and thinkers. My brothers, Larry and Fred, and my sister, Deb, have been my primary go-to team for a long time. Thanks for your love and support.

I learned my initial core values from my parents—love and courage from my mom and the value of hard work from my dad. I miss them both.

Thanks to my wife, Mary. Her great heart, unflagging support, and love has been my inspiration and joy beyond words and love too deep for telling. To my favorite skiing buddies, Dan and Brian, you guys have made your dad proud.

I need to thank my best friend, trail buddy, and coauthor, Steve Smith. Thanks, Buddy!

From Steve Smith

There are many people in my life who have kept me afloat and not crashing ashore—some who are still here and others that have passed. I thank you all, but these words seem inadequate repayment for that incalculable debt.

For those of you still trying to keep me from getting lost at sea: First, I'd like to acknowledge and thank my wife, Corinne, for her

The Value Equation

steadfast love and hope; she has supported me and allowed me to stray off the beaten path. A man cannot ask for any more.

I'd also like to thank my mother, Wanda, who has maintained a mom's patience to continually love her wayward son, wherever he has wandered in life. Many thanks to my children, Drew and Tara, for enduring the frequent fits of an apparently spontaneous and crazy father. You have both sparked my ideas and fantasy, and frequently lit that short fuse, often to your own personal embarrassment. Thank you, Richard and Victoria, you have both given me reason to hope for the future.

Garry—thanks, Bro . . . God's grace.

ABOUT GARRY KRUM

Founder, President, Chief Advisor, Family Man

Garry Krum is the founder and president of Agora Strategic Consulting, an advisory firm specializing in serving midsized companies to grow profit and harmonize their values and business strategy. Garry attended New York University, Stern School of Business, and has 37 years of public and private work in strategic merger and acquisition consulting experience. He has lent his entrepreneurial expertise at the Colorado State University School of Business. Garry lives in Fort Collins, Colorado. He enjoys traveling, hiking, climbing, and skiing with his family.

ABOUT STEVEN SMITH

Senior Strategic Advisor, Financial Manager, Horseman

Steven Smith is a Senior Strategic Advisor for Agora Strategic Consulting. Throughout a long career in the Navy, he was known as a financial and strategic planner. Steven received his MBA from UCLA, his Master of Science at the Naval Postgraduate School, and a Master of National Security and Strategic Studies degree from the Naval War College. As a CPA and DoD acquisition professional, his three decades of experience as a finance manager within the U.S. Navy give him vast expertise as he works with companies to create sustainable success. He lives in Cheyenne, Wyoming, with his wife, Corinne, their German Shepherd, Kaizo, and two horses, Dollar and Stinky.

ABOUT AGORA

Agora Strategic Consulting Group is a business development company based in Fort Collins, Colorado, that works with business leaders seeking to grow their companies dramatically. Their group of highly skilled and experienced consultants are located across the country and primarily serve companies with leaders who are interested in outside-the-box, creative thinking. They challenge their clients to develop value-aligned business strategies to create personal and business success. They provide strategic consulting services using the Value Equation process in business development, business transition/exit planning, business acquisitions, and business assessments. They also use the Value Equation process as the backbone for Agora Transform Workshops, working closely with small groups of business owners and executives.

For more information about Agora and the team and services, please visit their website at AgoraConsulting.us.

VALUE EQUATION BUSINESS PLANNING

Agora's Value Equation process helps business owners and executives create significant growth by aligning their values and business strategies. As Agora guides you through the Value Equation process, it becomes clear the values which are important to instill within your company culture and the decisions that define your business. Once these key values are defined, they help to solidify business strategies that are clear to not only the entire company but clients and customers as well.

- Values and goal identification
- Business assessments
- Key Growth Factor planning
- Internal clarity and alignment
- Building organizational health
- Leadership development

Learn more at AgoraConsulting.us

ALOHA
PUBLISHING

AGORACONSULTING.US